Church Club of New York

Lauda Sion

Or, the Liturgical Hymns of the Church

Church Club of New York

Lauda Sion
Or, the Liturgical Hymns of the Church

ISBN/EAN: 9783744779104

Printed in Europe, USA, Canada, Australia, Japan

Cover: Foto ©Lupo / pixelio.de

More available books at **www.hansebooks.com**

Lauda Sion

OR

The Liturgical Hymns of the Church

Lectures

DELIVERED IN 1896 UNDER THE AUSPICES OF THE
CHURCH CLUB OF NEW YORK

NEW YORK
E. & J. B. YOUNG & CO.
COOPER UNION, FOURTH AVENUE
1896

COPYRIGHT, 1896
BY THE CHURCH CLUB OF NEW YORK

CONTENTS.

LECTURE I.

THE PSALTER 1

By the Rev. John P. Peters, D.D., Rector of St. Michael's Church, New York.

LECTURE II.

THE HYMNS OF THE EUCHARIST 49

By the Rt. Rev. Arthur C. A. Hall, D.D., Bishop of Vermont.

LECTURE III.

THE HYMNS OF THE DAILY OFFICES . . . 79

By the Rt. Rev. John Hazen White, D.D., Bishop of Indiana.

LECTURE IV.

THE HYMNS OF THE ORDINAL 121

By the Rt. Rev. Henry C. Potter, D.D., LL.D., D.C.L., Bishop of New York.

LECTURE V.

TE DEUM LAUDAMUS 163

By the Rev. William R. Huntington, D.D., Rector of Grace Church, New York.

The Psalter in the Jewish Church and in the Christian Church.

LECTURE I.

REV. JOHN P. PETERS, D.D.,
Rector of St. Michael's Church, New York.

THE PSALTER IN THE JEWISH CHURCH AND IN THE CHRISTIAN CHURCH.

There is a difficulty that meets us in the study of the Hebrew Psalms as poetry which does not meet us in the study of the classical productions of Greek and Latin authors, much less in the study of the masterpieces of modern European lyric poetry. It is possible to render into English verse a Spanish, or a French, or a German, or even a Latin or a Greek poem, in such a manner that the reader who does not understand these languages may obtain a fair conception of the sound and metre, as well as of the sense of the original, because the metrical canons of these languages, and the thought processes of the people who use them, have some resemblance to our own. But with Hebrew the case is different. The genius of the language is entirely unlike that of our own; the thought processes of the people who used it are altogether alien to us, and the metrical system is quite different from anything which we recognize as constituting poetical form, if, possibly, we except some of the much-admired and much-scoffed-at poetry of the school of Walt Whitman.

The essential form feature of Hebrew poetry is not measure, nor rhyme, nor even, as in Anglo-Saxon poetry, alliteration, but parallelism, that is, the repetition in form or substance, or both, of something already said. Not that measure, or rhyme, or alliteration are unknown to Hebrew poetry, but that none of these is formulated; none plays an essential part in the conception of that poetry.

Hebrew poetry is rhythmical, and it pleases the ear by the repetition of similar sounds, but its rhythm is too irregular to be metre or to be measured by quantities and syllables, and its repetition of similar sounds is neither rhyme nor alliteration, being quite without rule. Moreover, the rhythm and the assonance are subsidiary to the parallelism of line with line, which is the only approximately regular feature of Hebrew poetry. But even in its treatment of parallelism Hebrew poetry never developed a real system of prosody, but always maintained its primitive character, unhampered by fixed rules. So Ewald says: "The old Hebrew poetry, if not so rich and varied as that of the Indians and Greeks, has on the other hand a simplicity and transparency hardly to be found elsewhere, a natural sublimity which as yet knows little of art, and even where art comes into play lets it remain as it were unconscious and careless. Compared with the poetry of other ancient peoples, it appears as of a yet more simple and youthful age of mankind, overflowing with an internal fulness and grace, and as yet but little troubled about external ornament and nice artistic law." * But in quoting these words of Ewald's, and calling attention to the artlessness and lack of form of Hebrew poetry, I do not mean to say that it is therefore lacking in beauty. So far is this from being the case that some of the Hebrew lyrics are among the most beautiful ever composed in any tongue. Indeed, there have been literary

---

* It may be said in passing, that since Ewald's day we have learned that the Babylonians and Egyptians both composed their poetry on the same model as the Hebrews, and, as far as we know, these are the only three peoples which have made parallelism the essential feature of poetry, treating rhyme, metre, alliteration and assonance as subsidiary features only.

critics who have claimed that a few of the gems of Hebrew lyric song, such as the forty-second Psalm, for instance, " Like as the hart desireth the water brooks, so longeth my soul after thee, O God," are superior to any lyric poetry ever written, not excepting that of the Greeks.

Because Hebrew poetry thus remained always near its sources, therefore it did not develop the more elaborate poetical genera, such as the drama and the epos—although we have the beginnings of both—clinging rather to song poetry and to proverbs. Instead of the epic poem we have the tale told in prose interspersed with songs. Instead of the drama we have merely a combination of lyric and didactic verses. Even the prophets began to prophesy in song. Later they developed a sort of recitative rhythm, and some fell into prose; but the recitative rhythm, and even the prose, were always varied with lyrical outbursts.

Relatively speaking, but a small portion of Hebrew song poetry has come down to us. We have evidence of the existence of a body of popular secular song poetry which has been almost entirely lost, only a few small fragments having been preserved to us, such as the Song of Songs; the forty-fifth Psalm, which is a wedding hymn; the riddles of Samson; a few snatches of harvest songs preserved by the prophets; and a few folk songs, battle songs, and dirges scattered here and there through the historical and prophetical books. The names or first lines of a few popular songs are preserved in the headings of certain psalms, which were appointed to be sung to the tunes of those songs. So the twenty-second Psalm is set to the "Hind of the Dawn;" the forty-fifth Psalm is set to "Lilies;" the fifty-sixth Psalm to "The Dove of the Distant Terebinths;" the fifty-eighth, fifty-ninth, and some others to "Destroy Not," a well-known harvest song, to which we also find references in the prophets; the sixtieth to "Lily, a Testimony;" the eightieth to "Lilies, a Testimony." We have a curious and interesting case of this preservation of the titles of old songs in the sixty-eighth Psalm, verses 12 to 14, in the Prayer Book version. As they stand, these verses, while each sentence is sufficiently intelligible in itself, make no sense, and have no connection either with what precedes or what follows. The preceding verse reads: "The Lord gave the word: great was the company of the preachers," or, to render literally, "women bearing good tidings." The following verses read literally as follows:

"Kings of hosts flee, they flee; while housewives divide the spoil."
"If ye dwell among dungheaps."
"Dove's wings covered with silver,
  Her pinions with glittering gold."
"When the Almighty scattered kings therein."
"It snoweth in Zalmon."
Each of these separate and unconnected sentences I take to be the first line or title of a song, one or all of which may be sung at this point in this great processional hymn. Accordingly, we have here by my count five first-lines or titles of songs.

But almost all of the lyric poetry which has been preserved to us is religious. It was preserved and handed down for its religious character and its spiritual value. The lyric poems which we have, therefore, are hymns, and by far the greater part of these hymns are collected in the Psalter, although there are outside of the Psalter not a few fine religious lyrics, such as the Song of Hannah, the Song of Moses, the Prayer of Habakkuk, and the like.

As the Psalter is a hymn-book, so the growth of the Psalter may be compared with the growth of modern hymn-books. The hymns contained in it are by no means of one age, and in the case of the older hymns probably none have come down to us in their original form. A psalm like the eighteenth, which contains the glorious picture of Jehovah riding upon the storm, and manifesting himself in hailstones and coals of fire, in the thunder peal and lightning flash, and which is ascribed to David, is probably to be referred to David as the original composer, but is not to be supposed to be in its present form the work of David. There is no better commentary on the growth of psalms like this in the ancient Jewish hymn-book than those grand hymns of the Christian Church, the Te Deum and the Gloria in Excelsis. These have grown and changed, and we hardly know when they began, nor can we say that in their present form they were composed by any one man and scarcely even by any one age. They are the work of the Church, and the same is true of the great hymns of the Jewish Psalter, or at least of the hymns contained in the earlier books, which are the oldest hymns.

The Psalter as we now have it was the hymn-book of the second Temple, and was edited as such, that is, as the authorized hymnal of the Jewish Church, probably somewhere about 150 B.C. But there was behind that a period of growth of something like eight hundred and fifty years. This completed hymnal contains in itself a number of smaller collections, or fragments of collections. It is divided into five books, each of which concludes with a short doxology, excepting the last, which closes the whole collection with a grand Psalm of Praise. The first book ends with the forty-first Psalm; the second with the seventy-third; the third with the eighty-ninth; and the fourth with the one hundred and sixth Psalm. In our Prayer Book Psalter, and in the King James version of the Bible, the doxologies at the close of the books are treated as though they were a part of the psalms which they follow, and the divisions into books are not indicated. In the Canterbury version the divisions into books are marked, and the doxologies are separated somewhat from the psalms to which they are attached. Here is the doxology of the first book, which is printed as the 13th verse of the forty-first Psalm in the Prayer Book Psalter: "Blessed be the Lord, the God of Israel, from everlasting and to everlasting. Amen, and Amen."

This division into five books is, however, late and artificial, designed to bring the Psalter into harmony with the Pentateuch, and does not altogether represent the original collections. There are, properly speaking, three books of the psalms, and not five, the second and third books forming properly one whole, and the fourth and fifth books another whole. The earliest psalms and collections of psalms are contained in the first and the second and third books. None of these collections, as we now have it, goes back as far as the time of David, and probably the earliest does not, as a collection, antedate the Exile, although, as already pointed out, the basis of many of the psalms is Davidic. Before the time of David there were, I make no doubt, liturgical productions of psalm character intended for purposes of worship, but of these none has come down to us, unless it may be some scant fragments, such as the Song of the Ark, Numbers x. 35, 36:

"Arise, Jehovah; scattered be Thine enemies:
And let Thy haters flee before Thee;"
the priestly benediction, Numbers vi. 24-27:
"Jehovah bless thee, and keep thee;
Jehovah make His face to shine upon thee, and be gracious unto thee;
"Jehovah lift up His countenance upon thee, and give thee peace;"
The Song of Saul and David, 1 Samuel viii. 7:

"Saul hath slain his thousands, and David his ten thousands," etc.

David seems in some way to have organized the religious lyric poetry of the Hebrews, so that succeeding generations looked to him as the founder of psalmody. Later poets paraphrased his psalms, or portions of them, or composed new psalms in the Davidic spirit or after the Davidic method, somewhat in the same way in which modern poets have taken a theme from David and enlarged upon it, building an entire poem out of a single verse. All such psalms are naturally referred to David.

As time went on, the liberty of referring psalms to his name was extended. We see this in the Psalter itself, where the one hundred and eighth Psalm, a composite psalm composed by someone out of portions of the fifty-sixth and sixtieth Psalms, is called a Psalm of David. This custom is still better illustrated in the sixteenth chapter of the first book of Chronicles, where, in describing the instalment of the Ark in the midst of the tent that David had pitched for it, we are told that David ordained "to give thanks unto the Lord by the hand of Asaph and his brethren," and a long psalm is given therewith which is entirely composite, made up of portions of late psalms, namely, the one hundred and fifth, the ninety-sixth, and the one hundred and sixth, psalms composed many centuries after the time of David, and not ascribed to him in the Psalter. Perhaps, however, the most instructive example of this method of composing psalms under the name of David, is the additional Psalm, one hundred and fifty-one, added at the close of the Septuagint Psalter, with this superscription: "This is the psalm written by his own hand of David, and outside of the number, when he fought Goliath." It is a psalm composed of scraps of other psalms.

But this use of the name of David in connection with the Psalter is, on the other hand, an evidence of the predominant part which he played in the organization of the Temple minstrelsy and the establishment of psalm poetry.

To return to the collection of the psalms as we have them, it should be understood, to begin with, that they are put together, generally, in the order of composition, and that therefore the earliest psalms are to be found in the earliest books. We must look for the psalms which are in the literal sense "Psalms of David" chiefly, if not altogether, in the first book. This book may be said to constitute the first collection of

Psalms for Temple use of which we have a certain record. With the exception of the first and second Psalms, which were prefixed to the collection at a later date, the tenth Psalm, which is properly a part of the ninth, and the thirty-third, which was attached to the thirty-second as a part of that psalm, all the psalms of this book are designated as Psalms of David. That is, this book was once one collection called "The Psalms of David," or the like. There are indications that this collection was composed out of more than one earlier collection, but these indications are not absolutely clear, and the earlier collections have been so handled in the composition of this larger collection that neither their date nor their limits are clearly ascertainable.

The second and third books comprise several distinct collections which can be clearly distinguished by their headings. There is here also a Psalter of David, which consists of Psalms fifty-one to seventy-two. The title of these psalms is given in a verse following the doxology attached to the seventy-second Psalm, and numbered in our Bibles verse 20: "The prayers of David, the son of Jesse, are ended." Psalms forty-two to forty-nine are a Psalter of the sons of Korah. Psalms one and seventy-three to eighty-three, are a Psalter of Asaph. At a later time, after these collections had been put together, they were disjointed by accident or by intention, and we have one Psalm of Asaph preceding the Psalter of David, and the rest following it. These three collections were afterwards edited and formed into one whole with the addition of Psalms eighty-five to eighty-nine, which come not only from different hands, but also from a different school. In Psalms forty-two to eighty-three, as originally existing, the name used for God had been Elohim. The composers or compilers of these additional Psalms, eighty-four to eighty-nine, used the name Yahweh, or Jehovah. It is evident, moreover, that the same persons not only added these psalms, but also edited the psalms of the other collections in these two books, from the fact that in the extra verses and choruses which have been inserted or appended here and there, the name Yahweh is used, instead of Elohim. It is interesting to observe that one of the psalms of this collection, Psalm fifty-three, is the same as Psalm fourteen of the first book of the Psalter, with the exception only that Psalm fifty-three uses the name Elohim for God, while Psalm fourteen uses the name Yahweh. There are also some slight textual differences in the two forms of the psalm, which amount merely to variant readings.

The psalms up to this point, to the close of the eighty-ninth Psalm, or the end of the third book, are provided quite freely with musical notes, and also with historical headings. But from the ninetieth Psalm on there is no musical annotation of the character of that prefixed to the psalms in the earlier books, and there are comparatively few historical headings.

Everyone who has read the psalms in the King James version will remember the curious headings prefixed to some of them. Beginning with the fourth Psalm a large number are headed, "To the chief musician," or, as the marginal reading has it, "To the overseer." This same fourth Psalm, which is an evening hymn, is "On Neginoth." The fifth Psalm, according to the King James version, "Is to the chief musician on Nehiloth." The sixth Psalm is to the chief musician "On Neginoth upon Sheminith," for which is substituted in the margin "upon the eighth." The seventh Psalm is a "Shiggaion of David," etc.

If you should turn to the revised version, you would find the fourth Psalm described as " For the chief musician on stringed instruments;" while the fifth Psalm is "for the chief musician on Nehiloth," and in the margin, "wind instruments." The sixth Psalm is, "for the chief musician on stringed instruments" set "To Sheminith," in the margin, "the eighth." The seventh Psalm is still the "Shiggaion of David."

These are apparently notes with regard to the musical accompaniment of the Psalms and the like. I have already pointed out that in some cases the catch-words of tunes are also given. But at an early date these musical, or liturgical directions became unintelligible through the change, possibly, of the musical system of the Hebrews. At all events, when the Psalms were translated into Greek, somewhere, presumably, in the second century before Christ, these musical instructions were no longer intelligible. Some of the translations of the musical directions in the "Septuagint," or Greek translation of the Psalter, are even quite ludicrous. What our translators render "to the chief musician," the Greek translators render always "unto the end." Where in the heading of the fifth and sixth Psalms our translators have rendered either "with the Nehiloth," simply transferring the Hebrew word without translating it, or with "wind instruments," the Greek has translated, " In behalf of the woman inheriting."

Now the reason why there are no such musical headings from the ninetieth Psalm onward seems to be that before the time of the collection of the psalms in the fourth and fifth books the musical system had undergone a change, and the later terminology had become as unintelligible to the Jews as it now is to us. Reverence for what had come down from the fathers led to the retention of those unintelligible terms in the psalm collections which had already been made, but they were not used in the new collections.

With regard to the historical headings, the case is somewhat different. We can observe those headings in process of growth. They are in the Hebrew text particularly numerous in the collection of " The Prayers of David, son of Jesse," Psalms fifty-one to seventy-two, inclusive. Here, as in the first book of psalms, where historical headings have been prefixed, the historical notes are all taken out of the books of Samuel.

Taking up the Greek translation of the Psalter, we find that the historical headings are much more numerous there than in the Hebrew

Psalter, and refer to many more circumstances in the life of David. The Davidic origin of the psalms was making itself felt as the generations went on in the application by later commentators of individual psalms to particular events in the life of David.

But to return to the collections of psalms. Not only do we observe this sharp distinction between the psalms before ninety and after ninety in regard to musical notation: there is a similar difference in other matters also. The psalms from three to eighty-nine are, I think, without exception psalms which have grown in the mouth of the people. Take for instance Psalms nine and ten, which really constitute one whole, and are divided into two by some accident in that particular text from which our modern Hebrew texts are descended. This psalm constituted originally an alphabetic acrostic. The first verse begins with the first letter of the alphabet, the third with the second letter, the fifth with the third, etc. It was a psalm not exactly of the exultant type, but certainly not representing any very great feeling of calamity. At a later date the verses between K and Q were cut out and other verses, not acrostic, and of most mournful character, were substituted in their stead. So that the psalm as it comes down to us is a Jeremiad.

This method of adapting psalms to circumstances is even more noticeable in the case of the forty-fourth Psalm. This psalm, as I think anyone will see if he will examine his Psalter carefully, ended originally with the eighth verse, the ninth verse in the Prayer Book Psalter, at which point in the King James version, as also in the Canterbury revision, you will find a *selah*, another of those Hebrew musical terms of which the meaning was early lost. It is a glorious, bright psalm, a psalm of triumph and of victory.

1. We have heard with our ears, O God, our fathers have told us: what thou hast done in their time of old:

2. How thou hast driven out the heathen with thy hand, and planted them in: how thou hast destroyed the nations, and cast them out.

3. For they gat not the land in possession through their own sword: neither was it their own arm that helped them:

4. But thy right hand, and thine arm, and the light of thy countenance: because thou hadst a favor unto them.

5. Thou art my King, O God: send help unto Jacob.

6. Through thee will we overthrow our enemies: and in thy Name will we tread them under that rise up against us.

7. For I will not trust in my bow: it is not my sword that shall help me:

8. But it is thou that savest us from our enemies: and puttest them to confusion that hate us.

9. We make our boast of God all day long: and will praise thy Name for ever.

But the ninth verse, the tenth according to the Prayer Book version, begins a very wail of distress, contrasting the former triumph and exultation with the present misery and oppression.

Another example of the method in which the Psalter grew in the mouth of the Jewish Church is the nineteenth Psalm. Here are joined together a very beautiful short-metre, quick-moving psalm, describing the glory of God as exhibited in the daily course of the sun, and a long-metre psalm, of a curious and somewhat limping verse, singing the praise of the law of God. The two make a beautiful combination in thought, although in the Hebrew text the metres are in most curious and surprising contrast, setting forth the glory of God as displayed equally in

His outward world, and in the inner world of the heart of man. God's sun gives light to one, Jehovah's law lighteneth the other.

All through these books the Church speaks. The individual who composed the psalm, whoever he may be, whether David or some later writer, has in the course of time been eliminated, and you have not the thought of any one individual, or the experience of any one individual, but the thought and the experience of the Church.

But although used by the Church, these psalms, in many cases at least, bear evidence of not having been composed originally for the Temple service. So the twentieth and the twenty-first Psalms are both battle hymns, or rather the twentieth is the hymn of the king going out to battle, and the twenty-first a Te Deum after victory. The forty-fifth Psalm, as we are told in the heading, is a " song of loves," that is, it was written originally as an epithalamium, or marriage hymn.

Now beginning with the ninetieth Psalm we come into a somewhat different atmosphere. The psalms of the fourth and fifth books are for the most part written for the express purpose of being sung in the service of the Temple. And yet this is not true of every psalm in the latter portion of the Psalter. There are here also a number of collections which have been joined together to make finally one whole. One of these is a collection of Folk Hymns.

If you will look at the psalms in your King James version, or in the Canterbury revision of the Bible, you will find that Psalms one hundred and twenty to one hundred and thirty-four, inclusive, bear in the King James version each the heading, " A song of degrees," and in the Canterbury revision " A song of ascents." They are really a " Pilgrim Psalter," sung by the Pilgrims who came up to Jerusalem from the " captivity," the name, which, even after the return from the exile, was applied to those Jews who continued to reside in Babylonia. Some of these psalms are among the most beautiful in the Psalter. If you will read them with a recollection of their origin and first use, I think, so vivid are their pictures, that you can almost imagine yourself marching, marching with those pilgrims over the boundless plain, out of the land of idolatry up toward the mountains whence cometh their help, in which, encircled by hills, is the holy city, Jerusalem, " built as a city that is at unity in itself," whither " the tribes go up, even the tribes of the Lord." The poetry of these psalms, with the exception of the one hundred and thirty-second, is different from the poetry of any other portion of the Psalter. They are full, moreover, of dialectical peculiarities and of Babylonianisms, which indicate their origin among the Jews of the captivity. Apparently, after they had sung themselves into the heart of the people, used generation after generation by the Jews of the dispersion on their pilgrimages to Jerusalem, they were adopted by the collectors of a new Psalter, and incorporated in that collection.

Among the most characteristic of the collections in the later portion of the Psalter is the Praise of the Law, the one hundred and nineteenth Psalm, which is really twenty-two psalms in itself, consisting of that number of divisions, each verse of which begins with one certain letter of the alphabet, so that the whole psalm is an alphabetic acrostic, with each letter repeated eight times over, while each verse contains some name of the law, and some attribute of the law. Characteristic also are the Hallel or Hallelujah collections. One of these Hallelujah collections consists of Psalms one hundred and eleven to one hundred and seventeen, inclusive. These psalms, with the addition of the one hundred and eighteenth, constitute the Hallel, which was sung by the Jews at the Passover, as the Songs of Degrees were sung at the Feast of Tabernacles. Another Hallel or Praise collection is that which closes the entire collection of Psalms, namely, Psalms one hundred and forty-six to one hundred and fifty, inclusive.

I might go much further into details, and might endeavor to set before you some theory as to the dates of these collections of psalms, and of the manner in which they were put together, but I trust that I have said enough to show the composite character of the Psalter and its slow growth, its use in the mouth of the people, and its adaptations to the needs of God's people, as those needs came upon them; enough to show you that it was the expression of the spiritual life of the chosen people of God for almost one thousand years; and enough to show you why it has continued from that date to this the unsurpassed and unsurpassable Hymn-book of the Church.

And now let us ask ourselves what we know about the liturgical or ritual use of the Psalter among the Hebrews. I have already pointed out that by the heading of the forty-fifth Psalm we are informed that that psalm was at some time a wedding hymn, and indeed a study of the psalm itself makes it clear that this was the purpose for which it was composed. The heading of the one hundred and second Psalm reads as follows: " A Prayer of the afflicted, when he is overwhelmed, and poureth out his soul before Jehovah." In other words, the one hundred and second Psalm was a penitential psalm, appointed to be used by persons in distress of mind or body. In the headings of Psalms thirty-eight and seventy you will find, in the Canterbury version, the words: " To bring to remembrance," and in the margin the alternative rendering: " To make memorial." But the word so translated means literally " to make *askara.*" Now the askara was that part of the meal or vegetable offering, called " meat offering " in the authorized translation of the Bible, which was cast into the sacrificial fire as God's portion. This is a liturgical note, then, informing us that at some time these psalms were appointed to be used in the Temple in connection with the sacrifice or office of the *askara.*

A rubric incorporated in the one hundred and eighteenth Psalm gives us a clew to the use of that processional hymn. If you will turn to the twenty-seventh verse of that psalm in the Prayer Book version, you will see that the second half reads: " Bind the sacrifice with cords, yea, even unto the horns of the altar." Now, in the Hebrew that is in prose, while both what precedes and what follows are poetry. This is, then, manifestly not a half verse of the psalm; but a rubrical direction that at this point the sacrifice should be bound to the horns of the altar preparatory to its slaughter. The one hundred and eighteenth Psalm was a processional hymn to be used on the occasion of a grand and festive sacrifice.

The use of some psalms is marked by their contents. Psalm three is a morning hymn, Psalm four an evening hymn, used at some period for the morning and evening service in the Temple. (Unfortunately in our present arrangement of the Psalter we sing Psalm four, the evening hymn, in the morning.) Psalm twenty-four was a processional hymn; Psalm sixty-seven a harvest hymn, etc.

One of the psalms in the later collections, Psalm ninety-two, is headed: " A Psalm, a song for the Sabbath-day." That is to say, this psalm was appointed to be sung in the sacrificial service in the Temple on the Sabbath. The Hebrew text of the psalms gives us no evidence of the appointment of special psalms for the other days of the week, but in the Greek translation, the Septuagint, we find by the headings that the twenty-fourth Psalm was appointed for Sunday, the forty-eighth for Monday, the eighty-second for Tuesday, the ninety-fourth for Wednesday, the eighty-first for Thursday, and the ninety-third for Friday; information which the Talmud confirms. In the time of our Lord these psalms constituted the regular psalters for the service of the daily morning sacrifice in the Jewish Temple, and were sung week in and week out. But on certain special occasions special psalms were appointed to be used instead of the Psalter for the day, as for instance the eighty-first Psalm at morning sacrifice on the new moon of the seventh month, and the twenty-ninth at evening sacrifice on the same day. These selections were very short in comparison with our present use, but there were also occasions, as already stated, on which an entire group of psalms, like the eight psalms of the Hallel, or the fifteen psalms of Degrees, were appointed to be sung.

The Jews were in the habit of treating the psalms with a great deal of freedom for liturgical purposes, cutting them and compounding them to produce chants suitable to their purpose. When they used the Song of Moses, Deuteronomy xxxii., they divided it into six different chants, one of which was considered enough for one service, which reminds one of the manner in which the compilers of our Prayer Book have cut out the chants Bonum est and Benedic Anima Mea from Psalms ninety-two and one hundred and three. Psalm one hundred and eight is a chant composed of verses 6 to 12 of Psalm sixty and 8 to 12 of Psalm fifty-seven, in the same way in which the Venite in our Prayer Book is composed of verses 1 to 7 of Psalm ninety-five, and verses 9 and 13 of Psalm ninety-six. A still more interesting example of this method of composing new psalms or chants out of portions of others is afforded us in the Psalm of Dedication in the sixteenth chapter of the first book of Chronicles.

I have already called attention to the existence of glorias or doxologies in the psalms. One of these is used at the end of the chant in the sixteenth chapter of the first book of Chronicles; and, indeed, we may pretty fairly conclude that those doxologies were placed at the end of each collection of psalms, as we place doxologies at the end of our hymnals, to be sung not only after the psalms which they immediately follow, but after any psalm in the collection as it might be used. Some of the smaller collections of psalms in the Psalter have special doxologies of their own. So the one hundred and seventeenth Psalm, that very short two-versed psalm:

"O Praise the Lord, all ye heathen: praise him, all ye nations.
For his merciful kindness is ever more and more towards us; and the truth of the Lord endureth for ever. Praise the Lord,"

is the gloria to the Hallel; and the one hundred and thirty-fourth Psalm:

"Behold, now, praise the Lord: all ye servants of the Lord,
Ye that by night stand in the house of the Lord: even in the courts of the house of our God.
Lift up your hands in the sanctuary: and praise the Lord.
The Lord that made heaven and earth: give thee blessing out of Zion,"

to the Pilgrim Psalter, or Songs of Degrees.

But not only did the Jewish Church have the same method of using doxologies which we have now, and indeed which we adopted from them, they had also the same method of using the Amen, and the Hallelujah. So, at the close of the chant to which I have already referred in the sixteenth chapter of first Chronicles, we are told that all the people said Amen and Hallelujah, and at the close of the one hundred and sixth Psalm there is a rubric, unfortunately printed in both our Bibles and Prayer-books as a part of the psalm itself, to this effect, "And let all the people say Amen, Allelujah." It was the practice, in other words, at the close of the doxology to respond Amen. Hallelujah was similarly used, and when we use it before or after some of our praise hymns, especially in the Easter season, we are but copying the old Jewish use. In fact, the Amens and Hallelujahs which we find in the Psalter are not in general original parts of the psalms with which they are connected, but liturgical directions, if I may so express it, like the Amens which we sing at the close of our hymns.

To sum up in its main features our knowledge of the liturgical use of the Psalter among the Jews, we may say that the Jews had a daily Psalter arranged according to the week, not the month. They had special psalms for special festivals. They composed anthems by divisions and combinations of already existing psalms, as well as by new compositions. They sung a gloria at the close of each chant or anthem. Glorias were also sung at the close of each selection of psalms used in a service. They made use after the Gloria of the response, Amen. They used, liturgically, sometimes at the close of their hymns, and sometimes at the beginning, the ascription of praise, Hallelujah, that is, " Praise ye the Lord."

Now it must not be supposed that after the close of the Psalter the Hebrews ceased to compose psalms or hymns on the ancient models. At the time of our Lord they were still composing such psalms. One collection, entitled, " The Psalter of Solomon," which was collected not many years before our Lord's birth, has come down to our own time. At a much later date the form of Hebrew poetry changed entirely, becoming rhymed, and there are in the modern Jewish rituals many beautiful hymns of rhymed poetry. But no psalm and no hymn composed after the final collection of the Psalter, somewhere about 150 B.C., was admitted into the sacred collection, however highly it might be esteemed. Such later hymns, used in their ritual, but not contained in the Psalter, you might compare with our Te Deum, Gloria in Excelsis, and Ter Sanctus, which we practically treat as inspired, and which the people reverence equally with the Psalter, but which cannot be admitted into the sacred collection, and are therefore technically placed upon a different plane.

The Christian Church inherited the Psalter from the Jewish Church, and the earlier Christians not only continued to use the Psalter as their Hymn-book, but also adopted its spirit and began to compose new psalms as the Jews had done before them. Four of these, the "Magnificat," "Nunc dimittis," "Angelic Hymn," and "Benedictus" are contained in our New Testament. Others of a later date, but formed on the same model, like the "Te Deum," although not contained in the Bible, hold in the liturgy of the Church a position of honor equal with the Psalms and Gospel Hymns.

There have come down to us besides these hymns, which we have incorporated in our New Testament, or our ritual, other fragments of early Christian psalms and odes, composed on psalm models, which show us that in the first Christian centuries the Psalter was a living force, and the spirit of psalmody not yet extinct.

As far as we can learn, the Christians at first

followed in their liturgies the Jewish use of the Psalter, almost, if not quite, in its entirety. In form the Christian liturgy was founded on the Jewish in every detail, and the earliest Christian litany which we find, our familiar,

" Lord have mercy upon us,
Christ have mercy upon us,
Lord have mercy upon us,"

is but an adaptation of the synagogue litany, or responsive prayer, adapted from the fifty-first Psalm. Regular psalms, or selections of psalms, were appointed for the days of the week, a song of gladness for the first day, a song of sorrow and mourning for the sixth day; and similarly for the great feasts and fasts. In the Sunday service one psalm, or a portion of a psalm, or an anthem made out of selections from the psalms was sung, or, perhaps, on some special occasion several psalms were united to form a selection, and sung over one Gloria. At the end of each selection, whether composed of one psalm, a portion of a psalm, or a group of psalms, the Gloria was sung, after the Jewish custom, and so universal did this use of the doxology or Gloria soon become that at a very early date a doxology was added even to the Lord's Prayer, and many manuscripts of St. Matthew's Gospel give it with that doxology, " For thine is the kingdom, the power and the glory, for ever and ever, Amen," as though this were a part of the prayer itself.

It is in the fourth and fifth centuries after Christ that we find liturgies beginning to assume definite and fixed forms. By that time the Bible had ceased to be the live book which it had been to the earlier Christians, and was beginning to receive a more mechanical treatment. With the growing lack of comprehension of the sense of Scriptures there went hand in hand an increase of reverence for the name and form, so that mere repetition of Bible words came to be regarded as in itself meritorious. This showed itself most of all in the treatment of the Psalter, which was best adapted of all parts of Scripture to memorizing, and had from the beginning been memorized more freely than other portions of the Bible, so that, we are told, it was not uncommon to find devout laymen who could recite the Psalter through from the beginning to the end, while children began their study of the Bible with the Psalter.

At this time we begin to find some slight distinctions between the Eastern and the Western use. The Eastern Church clung somewhat more closely than the Western to the Jewish and earlier Christian method of singing the Psalter. The Gloria was used only at the end of each selection of psalms, and not at the end of each individual psalm, while in the Western Church it had already become the custom to put the Gloria after everything, so that every individual psalm used in the service was followed by a Gloria, never mind how many psalms might follow one another. In the Eastern Church the early practice of selections, adaptations, the use of parts of psalms and the like, was still somewhat retained. In the Western Church the psalms, as is indicated, among other things, by the use of the Gloria just referred to, had come to be treated as individual wholes, which it was not allowable to change or modify in any manner. The Western Church had also developed more fully, it would appear, the idea of using the psalms consecutively in the order in which they chance to stand in the Psalter.

In both Eastern and Western churches there grew up gradually the practice of interspersing antiphons or anthems through the psalms and Scripture readings. This practice grew with the growing ignorance of the contents of the Bible, until at last, in the period of the densest ignorance of the Latin Church, it was the custom to sing an antiphon after each verse of each psalm. As the number of psalms used in each service was continually on the increase, owing to the idea that there was a merit in reciting as many psalms daily as possible, the Psalter of the daily services finally reached an inordinate and impossible length. Fancy eighteen psalms sung in one service, and these more than doubled in length by the insertion of an antiphon after each verse and the addition of a gloria at the close of each psalm.

It was the predominance of monasticism and the development of the hour services in the Latin Church that brought about the use and abuse which I have just noticed. It had become the rule to sing the Psalter through each week, and at certain seasons more frequently. There was a virtue in the mere repetition of the words, and to sing the whole Psalter through each week had a value in itself quite apart from an intelligent comprehension of the service rendered, or an intelligent participation in that service. About twelve psalms, increasing at one time to eighteen, as noted above, were appointed as the selection for each service, interspersed with antiphons, and with a gloria after each psalm. Nevertheless, the older practice of selections for special festivals so far prevailed that the psalms were not arranged for use altogether according to the order of their position in the Psalter. The fourth Psalm, which is an evening hymn, was recognized as such, and appointed to be used at evening service, while the third Psalm, which is the corresponding morning hymn, was appointed for the morning; the ninety-fifth Psalm, the Venite, was removed altogether from the regular course, and treated as an introduction to the entire service of psalmody for the day, following an early Christian use; psalms like the fifty-first, the Miserere, were appointed for fast days, etc. As the number of saints' and special days and the observance of those days increased, so the system of selections was developed, until at last the selections practically took the place of the regular daily Psalter in the monastic hour services, in which there was, from the point of view of the monks, a practical advantage, inasmuch as the selections were shorter than the regular portions.

At the time of the Reformation then the entire Psalter was theoretically sung or recited once a week, excepting only such psalms of special use as the fourth, fifty-first, ninety-fifth, etc., which were used many times over, but in actual practice only two-thirds of the psalms were really in use, selected and arranged in special services. This the reformers within the Roman Church regarded as an abuse adopted for the sake of ease and convenience, demanding instead the use of the entire Psalter weekly.

The fathers of the English Reformation adopted the theory of the mediæval Roman use contended for by these reformers, namely that the whole Psalter should be sung through, and seem to have regarded all deviations from the regular order through the use of special psalms for holy days as an abuse to be corrected. They stood for the study and use by the people of the whole Bible, and not merely of selected portions, and in the matter of the psalms it seemed to them desirable that the whole book should in some manner be put in the mouth of the people. No other way was so well adapted to make them familiar with the whole Psalter as to have it read through in order. Moreover, partly owing to the development of a modern hymn poetry totally unlike that of the psalms and the early hymns of the Christian Church founded on psalm models, such as the Te Deum, the Gloria in Excelsis, etc., the use of which made them think that the psalms were not hymns, and partly because of their way of looking at the Bible, the reformers had come to regard the psalms as a collection of inspired texts, wholesome to be read, rather than as hymns intended to be sung as such; for chanting was regarded as a form of reciting rather than a real singing.

But with the best intentions it was impossible under the new order either to say or to sing the whole Psalter through once a week. Consequently, in order to carry out this new theory of saying the whole Psalter through in order from beginning to end, they were compelled to abandon the ancient Catholic plan of the arrangement of the psalms according to a weekly cycle, which the Christian Church had inherited from the Jewish, and which prevailed everywhere, east and west alike, and to substitute a monthly arrangement, a thing hitherto unheard of in Christendom. For only some half dozen of the greatest feasts of the Church did they appoint special psalms, for the other three hundred and fifty-nine days of the year, Sundays and week days, feast days and fast days, they ordered that the psalms should be said in rotation, with no reference whatsoever to Church seasons or the lesson of the day. Friday psalms might fall on Sunday and Sunday psalms on Friday; henceforth all this was left to chance. The important thing was to have the whole Psalter said through at frequent intervals. Accordingly the Psalter was divided into sixty sections, as nearly equal as they could be made without dividing individual psalms other than the one hundred and nineteenth. These divisions were allotted in order to the days of the month, two divisions being assigned to each day, one for the morning and one for the evening. The evening hymn, Psalm four, chanced to fall in the equal portion which had been cut off for the first morning, and in the morning it has therefore been said or sung ever since. Similarly the fact that the ninety-fifth Psalm chanced to fall in the thirty-eighth equal section made it a part of the Psalter for the nineteenth morning, quite regardless of the fact that as the Venite it constituted the introduction to the Psalter on every day of the year.

According to the Anglican arrangement, supposing a man to go to church twice a day during the whole year, he would read or sing each psalm twelve times over with the exception of a very few which he would use thirteen times, and a few more which he would use eleven times, while the Venite, or Psalm ninety-five, he would repeat three hundred and sixty-four times. If he go to church twice each Sunday, and twice on the four days not Sundays for which special psalms are appointed, during the year 1896, he will use every psalm but the one hundred and sixteenth, one hundred and seventeenth, and the first four divisions of the one hundred and nineteenth Psalm. If, however, he go to church only once a Sunday, in the morning, and once on each of the four special psalm days not Sundays, also in the morning, he will have used one psalm, the ninety-fifth, fifty-five times, eleven psalms three times, thirty-eight psalms twice, forty-nine psalms once (counting each of the five sections of Psalm one hundred and nineteen as a separate psalm) and sixty-five psalms he will have altogether failed to use.

The compilers of the American Prayer Book, in 1789 and 1792, retained in general the peculiarities of the Anglican use of the psalms, but introduced some important modifications, conforming their use somewhat more to primitive Christian use. In addition to the regular Psalter for the day selections of psalms were provided and recommended for use, being printed before the Psalter, with a view to providing appropriate psalms for all seasons of the Church year, and especially for Sundays. In these selections, following primitive use, the fathers of the American Church did not hesitate to use portions of psalms as well as entire psalms. They also reverted to primitive use in recommending the use of the Gloria Patri only after each selection or group of psalms, instead of after each psalm. Further than this, several new canticles were prefixed to the Psalter for optional use on the great feast days, composed after the manner of various primitive models by putting together verses from several psalms. Following the same primitive freedom of treatment, the Venite was vastly improved by dropping verses 8 to 11 of Psalm ninety-five, and substituting therefor two verses, 9 and 13, of Psalm ninety-six. Two new canticles were also added to Evening Prayer, composed from psalms, but not consisting in either case of an entire psalm, the Bonum est, and the Benedic Anima Mea. A change was also made in the psalmody for the burial service on the same primitive model. The English Prayer Book provided two psalms, thirty-nine and ninety, each of which, after the Anglican manner, was to be used entire, and each to be followed by the Gloria. The American revisers omitted several somewhat irrelevant or inappropriate verses from each of these psalms, making of the two one anthem, and emphasized the unity of this, as over against the Anglican idea of separate psalms, by placing one Gloria at the end of the whole.

The late revision of our Prayer-book (1892) has in some directions advanced farther toward primitive models in the treatment of the Psalter, as in the increase in the number of the selections, and of the special psalms for special occasions, and in others it has receded toward the Anglican model; but in general practice there is little change. In fact, the ordinary American use of the Psalter may be said to be to-day, as it has always been, practically identical with the Anglican use.

I have confined myself to the questions of form and use in dealing with my subject, because the psalms are far too large a theme to cover in one lecture in all its aspects. I should have liked to have studied with you the occasion of the composition of some of the wonderful hymns of the Psalter, analyzed their beauties and followed their use not only in the Jewish, but also in the Christian Church, recalling the memories of good men and great deeds which are, as it were, entwined about them. David and Simon Maccabæus, the temple of Jerusalem and the temple of Dan, the triumph of Israel and its downfall, the captivity and the restoration, priests and prophets, Babylonians and Persians, Syrian oppressors and Maccabæan patriots all left their mark upon the Psalter. Out of the psalms speak all the vicissitudes of the life of the people of God for well-nigh a thousand years. And after the Psalter was finally closed as a collection of hymns, it still continued to live in the hearts and lives of the people of God. How many martyrs have not these psalms upheld in persecution, how many afflicted souls have they not consoled, how many feet have they not guided into the way of peace! They have comforted the dying as they passed through the valley of the shadow of death, and they have cheered armies to victory. Henry of Navarre made the sixty-eighth Psalm his battle hymn; and when on the 12th of September, 1683, John Sobieski descended from the heights of the Kahlenberg upon the hordes of the Turks besieging Vienna, his army chanted that magnificent Psalm, one hundred and fifteen:

Not unto us, Jehovah, not unto us,
But unto Thy name give glory,
Because of Thy love and Thy truth.
Why do the nations say :
" Where is then their God ? "
For our God is in heaven ;
He doth whatsoever He will.

Their idols are silver and gold,
The work of men's hands.
Mouths have they—and speak not ;
Eyes have they—and see not ;
Ears have they—and hear not ;
Noses have they—and smell not ;
With their hands—they touch not ;
With their feet—they walk not ;
Neither breathe they with their throat.
Like them shall they be that make them,
Whosoever doth trust in them.

O Israel, trust in Jehovah !
   He is their help and their shield.
House of Aaron, trust in Jehovah !
   He is their help and their shield.
Ye that fear Jehovah, trust in Jehovah !
   He is their help and their shield.

Jehovah hath been mindful of us ; He will bless—
   Will bless the house of Israel ;
   Will bless the house of Aaron ;
   Will bless them that fear Jehovah,
Small and great alike.

Jehovah give you increase,
   For you and for your children.

Blessed be ye of Jehovah,
    Maker of heaven and earth.
The heavens are Jehovah's heavens ;
    But the earth He gave to the children of men.

The dead praise not Jehovah,
They that go down into silence ;
But we will bless Jah
Henceforth and for ever.
Halleluiah !

The Hymns of the Eucharist.

LECTURE II.

THE RT. REV. A. C. A. HALL, D.D.,
Bishop of Vermont.

THE HYMNS OF THE EUCHARIST.

Fragments of hymns of the Apostolic Church are preserved to us embedded in the New Testament.* They are commonly introduced by St. Paul into his later epistles with the phrase, "Faithful is the saying"—the saying familiar to those whom he is addressing. For instance, in the first Epistle to Timothy there is a fragment of a hymn on Redemption, incorporated into our Eucharistic Service as one of the "Comfortable Words":

> "Christ Jesus
> came into the world
> to save sinners." †

The same epistle gives a hymn on our Lord's

---

* See Liddon's Bampton Lectures, vi., pp. 332, 333 (16th edition, 1892), where the Greek is printed in verse arrangement.
† 1 Tim. i. 15.

Incarnation and Triumph that might well be styled an Apostolic Carol:

> "Who was manifested in the flesh,
> justified in the spirit,
> beheld of angels,
> proclaimed to the nations,
> believed on in the world,
> received up into glory."*

In the second Epistle to Timothy we have a quotation from a hymn on the Glories of Martyrdom:

> "If we died with Him, we shall also live with Him;
> if we endure with Him, we shall also reign with Him;
> if we shall deny Him, He also will deny us;
> if we are faithless, He abideth faithful;
> He cannot deny Himself." †

In the Epistle to Titus, a hymn on the Way of Salvation:

> "But when the kindness of God our Saviour and His love toward man appeared,
> Not by works done in righteousness which we did ourselves,
> But according to His mercy, He saved us,
> Through the washing of regeneration and renewing of the Holy Ghost,

---

* 1 Tim. iii. 16. The reading ὅς instead of θεός, which is adopted by the Revised Version, makes little difference in the meaning. For the Pre-existence of the Person is implied in the verb "was manifested."

† 2 Tim. ii. 11–13.

THE HYMNS OF THE EUCHARIST. 53

> Which He poured out upon us richly, through Jesus Christ our Saviour,
> That being justified by His grace,
> We might be made heirs according to the hope of eternal life."*

Once more, in the Epistle to the Ephesians, St. Paul quotes words of a hymn on Baptism or Penitence, founded on a passage from Isaiah.† "Wherefore it [the hymn] saith:

> "'Awake, thou that sleepest,
> And arise from the dead,
> And Christ shall shine upon thee.'" ‡

These and similar "hymns and spiritual songs" (referred to, it may be noted, in Epistles to these same Asiatic churches,§ as sung in gatherings of the faithful) would most probably have been used in connection with the celebration of the Holy Eucharist, which was at once the great occasion for the assembly of the faithful, the distinctive and central act of Christian worship, and pre-eminently the Sacrifice of Praise and Thanksgiving.

---

* Tit. iii. 4–7.
† Isa. lx. 1.
‡ Eph. v. 14.
§ Eph. v. 19 ; Col. iii. 16. "Speaking to yourselves" probably refers to responsive singing. See Keble's *Eucharistical Adoration*, p. 48.

Material for other services, corresponding with what in later language we should call the Choir Offices, was already provided in the Psalter, though doubtless Christian additions were made thereto, as in our doxology. Distinctive Christian hymns would probably have at any rate their chief use in connection with distinctive Christian rites, as we find in the report of the practice of Christians in Asia Minor sent by the Pro-consul Pliny to the Emperor Trajan. The Christians were accustomed, he had learned, to meet on a stated day before light, and to sing among themselves responsively a hymn to Christ as God, and to bind themselves by an oath (or sacrament—the pledge was probably involved in the sacrament as we should use the word) not to commit any wickedness.*

The celebration of the Eucharist, I said, would naturally gather round itself Christian hymns. For the leading idea of the Sacrament of our Lord's Body and Blood was that expressed in this very title of the Eucharist, the Sacrifice of Praise and Thanksgiving.

Beside the spiritual Food thus given, and the

---

* Plin. Ep. lib. x. ep. 97. The passage is quoted by Liddon, Bampton Lectures, vii., p. 399 Note.

pledge of Brotherhood sealed in the common participation of the One Loaf,* a solemn pleading indeed is therein made of the merits of Christ's death—of His obedience unto death †— for the obtaining for those participating and for all His whole Church the remission of sins and all other benefits of His Passion. This aspect of the rite was fully recognized in the early Church; but above, or perhaps we may more truly say *behind* this, was the idea of triumphant exultation in the redemption wrought out for mankind by the Incarnation and victorious Passion of the Eternal Son of God, whose life-giving Death is proclaimed and set forth before Heaven and earth in the sacramental Breaking of the Bread.‡

Chrysostom's words express this, which was, I believe, the central conception of the early Christian Church, " The awful mysteries, laden with mighty salvation, are called Eucharist, because they are the commemoration of many benefits." §

The Lord Himself at the Institution " gave

---

* 1 Cor. xi. 17.
† Phil. ii. 8.
‡ 1 Cor. xi. 26 καταγγέλλετε.
§ Hom. xxv. in Matt. (Field's edition, vol. i., p. 363).

thanks" before He "blessed" the gifts.* As the High Priest of all creation, the First begotten by whom and for whom all things were made, He on behalf of all gave thanks to the Father—His and ours—for the manifestation of His love in the creation of the world, for the high destiny to which He designed mankind, for His forbearance with fallen man, and His love in devising means that His banished be not expelled from Him,† for the gift of His Son that whoso believeth in Him should not perish with the fallen world, but should have eternal life in fellowship with Himself. Thus (we may reverently assume) He gave thanks and offered Himself a willing sacrifice to His Father and for His brethren for the accomplishment of the Father's purpose in their redemption; in the gifts that He blessed offering then by His own voluntary act His Body to be broken, His Blood to be shed, in strife with the powers of evil, that so He might rescue His brethren, and having Himself overcome the sharpness of death, might open the kingdom of Heaven to all believers. He then "gave thanks" for the redemptive victory which

---

* St. Matt. xxvi. 27. See Meditation XII., with the appended Note, in *The Final Passover*, by the Rev. R. M. Benson, Vol. II., part I. (Longmans, 1895.)
† 2 Sam. xiv. 14.

THE HYMNS OF THE EUCHARIST. 57

He would achieve at so great a cost. How should we, as we show forth the victorious struggle to which He then dedicated Himself, give thanks at once with Him and to Him who loveth us and loosed us from our sins by His Blood! "Worthy indeed is the Lamb that hath been slain to receive the power, and riches, and wisdom, and might, and honour, and glory, and blessing; for Thou wast slain, and didst purchase unto God with Thy Blood men of every tribe, and tongue, and people, and nation, and madest them to be unto our God a kingdom and priests; and they reign upon the earth." *

The Eucharist of the Christian Church is the echo or the continuation of the Thanksgiving of her Lord and Head as He instituted the holy mysteries wherein His people would shew forth His victorious death until He came again. In the older Liturgies the verbal thanksgiving, compressed into short sentences in our Common and Proper Prefaces, was expanded at great length, recounting the benefits of Creation and of Redemption, and always reaching its climax in the *Sanctus* sung by all.†

---

* Rev. i. 5, v. 9–12.
† See the article "Preface" in the *Dictionary of Christian Antiquities.*

Part of one such Preface or Thanksgiving may be quoted as an illustration of the general rule. The Liturgy called after St. James, used at Jerusalem, is not only itself preserved, but we have also an explanation of it in St. Cyril's instructions to those preparing for admission to the Sacraments delivered in the Church of the Holy Sepulchre in the year 347.*

After the bidding of the priest, " Lift up your hearts " and " Let us give thanks unto the Lord," with their familiar responses (the same used in our Liturgy to-day as in that of Jerusalem in the fourth century), the Thanksgiving proceeds:

"It is very meet and right, becoming us and our duty, that we should praise Thee, and celebrate Thee with hymns, and give thanks unto Thee, the Maker of all creatures, visible and invisible, the Treasure of all good, the Fountain of life and immortality, the God and Lord of all things, whom the heavens and the heavens of heavens praise, and all the host of them; the sun and moon and the whole company of stars; the earth and sea, and all that are in them; the celestial congre-

---

* St. Cyril's Catechetical Lectures are translated in the Oxford Library of the Fathers, Vol. II. See Lect. XXIII.

gation of Jerusalem; the Church of the firstborn who are written in heaven; the spirits of just men and prophets; the souls of martyrs and apostles; angels and archangels, thrones and dominions, principalities and powers, the tremendous hosts, cherubim with many eyes, and seraphim with six wings, with two whereof they cover their faces, and with two their feet, and with two they fly, crying out incessantly one to another, and singing with loud voices the triumphal song of the majesty of Thy glory, ' Holy, Holy, Holy, Lord of hosts, heaven and earth are full of Thy glory. Hosanna in the highest. Blessed be He that cometh in the name of the Lord. Hosanna in the highest.' " *

The angelic intelligences are thought of, as in the representation of heavenly worship in the Apocalypse,† as joining with redeemed man in the praise of the Thrice Holy (whose almighty power is ever exercised according to infinite wisdom, and in perfect love) for the manifestation of His goodness.‡ " Worthy art Thou, our

---

* Translated in Bingham's *Christian Antiquities*, Vol. V., pp. 88, 89. See *Liturgies Eastern and Western*, by C. E. Hammond, p. 40.

† Rev. iv., v.

‡ This may be regarded as a more fundamental idea in the

Lord and our God, to receive the glory and the honour and the power: for Thou didst create all things, and because of Thy will they were, and were created." " Unto Him that sitteth on the throne, and unto the Lamb, be the blessing, and the honour, and the glory, and the dominion, for ever and ever. Amen."

What I desire particularly to emphasize, what the Hymns of the Eucharist naturally suggest, is *the joyous character of the Eucharistic worship*, as expressed in the very title of the rite, and as expressive of the joy of the Christian life.

Early Christians did not think of themselves as aliens from God needing to be reconciled; miserable sinners seeking mercy and pardon— this was not the chief aspect in which they regarded themselves. Reconciled they were by the Blood of Christ. Washed, sanctified, and justified in the name of the Lord Jesus, and by the Spirit of our God,* they had access with

---

Tersanctus than that of the Blessed Trinity. The song is echoed in the vision of St. John from the Old Testament vision of Isaiah. This earlier truth concerning the Character of God finds fuller expression in the later disclosures of distinctions within the Divine Being, which teach us to recognize the Son as the Personal Wisdom, and the Holy Spirit as the Personal Love, of the Father.

* 1 Cor. vi. 11.

boldness to the throne of grace as members of the Incarnate Son.* Accepted in Him the Beloved,† they did not plead His Death for the breaking down of barriers between themselves and God; they proclaimed it as having accomplished their deliverance, and as they thus made their boast therein, they claimed the fruits of that victory, the benefits of His Passion, calling forth its virtue, as they were afresh united with Him by feeding on His glorified Humanity.

The Eucharist is no repetition of the Sacrifice once offered; but its continual representation and commemoration, the appointed means for calling forth and applying its benefits.

Here, too, the Eucharist is a counterpart of the pleading of our Lord for us in Heaven. We are not (in spite of some popular hymns or devotional manuals) to think of Him—glorified at the Right Hand of the Father in Heaven—at the highest place, that is, of honour and of power —as in the ordinary sense praying for us, neither on bended knee nor by petition.‡ "He has entered into Heaven to appear in the presence

---

* Heb. iv. 16.
† Eph. i. 6.
‡ "Interpellat pro nobis Dominus non voce sed miseratione." Bede, quoted by Bishop Westcott, on 1 St. John ii. 2.

of God for us." * His very presence pleads. "He ever liveth to make intercession for us." † His mediation is not in the way of asking from the Father, but rather as dispensing, according to His knowledge of our needs and in answer to our prayers, the gifts that He has received, of which His glorified Manhood has been made the channel of communication. ‡

In harmony with what has been said it should be noted that in the great promises held out by our Lord to faithful prayer on the part of His disciples, He does not represent Himself as only presenting their prayers to Another; He is in His own Person the Object of Prayer; *He* receives and answers prayers.

He not only promises, "Verily, verily, I say unto you, If ye shall ask anything of the Father in My Name, He will give it you;" § but also, "Whatsoever ye shall ask in My Name, *that will I do*, that the Father may be glorified in the Son." ‖ So St. John in his epistle writes: "This is the boldness that we have toward Him (the

---

* Heb. ix. 24, ἐμφανισθῆναι ὑπὲρ ἡμῶν.
† Heb. vii. 25 ; Rom. viii. 34, ἐντυγχάνει ὑπὲρ ἡμῶν.
‡ See Fr. Benson's *The Final Passover*, Vol. II., Part I., pp. 337, *sq*.
§ St. John xvi. 20, comp. xv. 16.
‖ St. John xiv. 13.

Son of God), that, if we ask anything according to His will, *He heareth us.*" *

It will at once be felt how out of harmony with this view of the triumphant character of the Eucharistic rite (which is certainly the tone of our Consecration Prayer) are many of the devotions, in prose or rhyme, popularly used in connection with the Holy Communion. These too often (and from very different sources) take as a standpoint for Eucharistic contemplation the Cross of Calvary, with the penitent malefactor or the Magdalen as the typical worshipper, whereas in the Eucharist we are bidden "lift up our hearts" and join the heavenly worship of Angels and Saints, to whose company we have been admitted, realizing that we "*are* already come unto Mount Sion, and unto the city of the living God, the heavenly Jerusalem; and to innumerable hosts of angels; to the general assembly and Church of the first-born who are enrolled in Heaven; and to God the judge of all, and to the spirits of just men made perfect; and to Jesus the mediator of a new covenant, and to the Blood of sprinkling that speaketh better than that of Abel." †

---

* 1 St. John v. 14, 15.
† Heb. xii. 22-24.

Penitence should not be the dominant note in our approach to the Lord's Table any more than in our recitation of the Lord's Prayer. The " Our Father " is the prayer, the Eucharist is the worship, and both express the attitude of God's redeemed and accepted children. We may, alas, have fallen from our Baptismal position of grace and privilege. Penitence and Reconciliation are then to *precede* our Eucharistic worship. Even in the service itself, the general confession and absolution are provided before at the *Sursum Corda* we enter on the more solemn and jubilant portion of the rite. As in the Levitical rites, reconciliation, when necessary, through the Sin-offering and the Trespass-offering, must *prepare the way* for the Burnt-offering of " sweet savour " and the Peace-offering of a sacrificial feast, which finds its realization in the Christian Eucharist.*

Our continual Eucharists celebrated Sunday by Sunday, or more often, correspond with the *annual* Paschal solemnity of the Jewish Church. The *yearly* Passover was the joyful commemoration of the great deliverance from

---

* For the relation of the Levitical Sacrifices to the Christian Mysteries, see *The Worship of the Old Covenant*, by E. F. Willis.

Egypt by virtue of the *original* Paschal Sacrifice. *That* has its fulfilment in the redeeming Sacrifice of the Lamb wrought out once for all in the Passion, offered at His entrance into Heaven, and applied at our Baptism.* By our continual commemoration thereof we, as Israel, abide in the covenant with God, to which we have been admitted by *that* sacrifice whose virtue we continually call forth.

Two or three ritual points may be mentioned here as following on the principles we have considered.

(*a*) The celebration of the Holy Eucharist should be joyous. It betrays a miserable appreciation of the real character of the rite to denude its administration of musical and other ceremonial embellishments with which perhaps lesser offices of worship are celebrated.

(*b*) With this conception of the Sacrifice of Praise and Thanksgiving is seen to harmonize the custom of the early Church in many parts, preserved as the ordinary rule in the East, not to celebrate the holy mysteries on Fasting days, and in particular the instinctive feeling as to the

---

* Heb. x. 10, 12, 14, 19–22.

inappropriateness of Good Friday for the Eucharistic commemoration.

(c) The loss of the true Eucharistic idea is conspicuously felt in the change in modern from primitive rites for the celebration of the Holy Sacrament in connection with the Burial of the Faithful. While praying for the repose of the departed, and for the continual increase of their joy, the leading idea of the early Church in such rites was of Thanksgiving for what God had done for them and in them whose obsequies she celebrated. This, of course, was the more natural in days when Christian profession involved, if not martyrdom, at least the risk of distinct worldly loss. It was equally natural that as Christian lives became less unworldly, the note of triumph which had marked Christian deaths should grow more faint, and that the penitential side of burial services and of the pleading of our Lord's Sacrifice as a part thereof should become more prominent. But the attempt to banish every trace of joy from a Requiem Mass, as in the present Roman use, surely marks a declension both in Christian life, and in the conception of the meaning of the shewing forth of the Lord's Death.*

---

* The following anthem from the Russian Burial Service shows

In proportion as Christians have taken Christ's Death as a law of life, and have sought to make real their Baptism into His Death,* can the "shewing forth" His Death have its true meaning in connection with their burial. So far as they in life practically regarded His Death as a mere sacrifice of substitution, the natural thought in prayer and Eucharist on their behalf when they have departed will be that of pleading for those under sentence for mitigation of their punishment. If penitence can never be absent from our approach to God—until the time of the perfected restitution of all things— and most certainly not when we think of the

---

the combination of the ideas of penitence and praise in the older rites:

Give rest, O Christ, to Thy servant with Thy saints, where sorrow and pain are no more, neither sighing, but life everlasting.

Thou only art immortal, the Creator and Maker of men: but we are mortal, formed of the earth, and unto earth must we return: for so didst Thou ordain when Thou created me, saying, "Dust thou art, and unto dust shalt thou return." All we go down to the dust, and weeping o'er the grave we make our song: Alleluia! Alleluia! Alleluia!

Give rest, O Christ, to Thy servant with Thy saints, where sorrow and pain are no more, neither sighing, but life everlasting.

See the *Guardian* for April 1, 1896, p. 511; and the article, "Obsequies of the Dead," in *Dictionary of Christian Antiquities*, Vol. II., p. 1430.

* Rom. vi. 3, etc.

soul giving account of the deeds done in the body, yet surely if New Testament Christianity is real to us, penitence will not be the only or the dominant note—in our prayer for ourselves or for those who dead to the world live unto God.

All this, I trust, may be regarded as fairly suggested by the title which is given in the Greek Liturgies to the first of our great Eucharistic Hymns. The *Tersanctus* is styled the Triumphal (as well as the Seraphic) Hymn.* It always followed, or was sung in close connection with, the great Thanksgiving, which in words expressed the leading idea of the whole Sacramental rite.

Turning to the more particular consideration of the second great Eucharistic hymn in our Service, the *Gloria in Excelsis*, there are three or four points of interest connected with the

---

* See Hammond's *Liturgies*. Glossary under "Hymn," p. 380. The *Tersanctus* must be distinguished from the Trisagion, ἅγιος ὁ Θεός, ἅγιος ἰσχυρός, ἅγιος ἀθάνατος, ἐλέησον ἡμᾶς, which in the Liturgies of St. Chrysostom and of St. Mark is sung in connection with "The Little Entrance," or solemn bringing in of the Book of the Gospels. In the Roman ritual it is used in the service of "The Reproaches" on Good Friday, and still in the Greek form.

liturgical use of different portions of the hymn.*

1. The entire hymn (as we know it) is of Greek origin, perhaps translated into Latin by Hilary of Poictiers, to whom by many the composition of the greater part has been (without doubt erroneously) ascribed. It is found, with some variations from the ordinary form, in the Apostolical Constitutions under the title (in later manuscripts) of "A Morning Prayer." †

In the Alexandrian manuscript of the Bible, known to students as Codex A, preserved in the British Museum, which probably belongs to the fifth century, the *Gloria in Excelsis* is inserted after the Psalms with thirteen other hymns, mostly taken from Holy Scripture.‡ There, too, it is called "a Morning Hymn."

In Western as in Eastern books of devotion it is prescribed for morning, and especially for Sunday morning, use.

The early use of the hymn as a whole was not

---

* See *Dictionary of Christian Antiquities*, Vol. I., pp. 706, 707; and Scudamore's *Notitia Eucharistica*, Chapter x., Section vi.

† Bk. vii., ch. 47.

‡ These ᾠδαι are all given at the end of Vol. III. of Swete's *The Old Testament in Greek* (Cambridge University Press, 1894). To the *Gloria in Excelsis* are added verses, some of them forming part of the *Te Deum*, some of them taken from the Psalter.

connected with the Eucharist. Only the first and Scriptural sentence, the Angels' Song proper, is found in any Greek or Oriental Altar Service; and this is not common, nor does it always occupy the same place in the Liturgy. In the Nestorian Liturgy of the Holy Apostles * (which is as old as the beginning of the fifth century) this first sentence actually opens the service, being evidently intended in its place here, as in the introductory parts of other Liturgies, to foreshadow and welcome the coming of Christ in the Sacrament, as the heavenly host heralded His advent in the flesh.

> "Glory to God in the highest,
> and on earth peace,
> good-will towards men." †

That which the angels proclaimed as the object of the Incarnation of the Redeemer, we rejoice in as the result of His mission.

---

* *I. e.* SS. Adaeus and Maris. See Hammond's *Liturgies*, Introduction, p. xxii., and p. 267.

† It is noteworthy that while the manuscripts of St. Luke ii. 14 vary between εὐδοκία and εὐδοκίας, in the Hymn εὐδοκία is always found. *Dictionary of Christian Antiquities*, Vol. I., p. 737. For a short discussion of the two readings see Appendix C to *The Songs of the Holy Nativity*, by Canon Bernard. (Macmillan, 1895.)

THE HYMNS OF THE EUCHARIST. 71

In early Western Liturgies likewise probably this first sentence alone was sung, and in a corresponding place, near the beginning of the service, the remaining portion of the hymn being incorporated into the Eucharistic office at a later date, and the whole hymn then being sung (as now in the Roman use) in the place for which the opening sentence was naturally fitted.

When introduced into the Roman Liturgy, for a long period the hymn was reserved, it may be remarked, for occasions when a bishop celebrated the Sacrament. This distinction was not observed in Gallican rituals.

The whole hymn was so well established in the West by the beginning of the tenth century, that it was frequently " farsed " with interpolations specially appropriate (or considered so) to particular festivals.*

2. The third part of the hymn, " Thou only art holy, Thou only art the Lord, Thou only, O Christ, with the Holy Ghost, art most high in the glory of God the Father," corresponds closely with the response made by the people to the proclamation of the priest in the ancient liturgies, as he elevated the consecrated gifts,

---

* See *Notitia Eucharistica*, pp. 695, 696.

and cried, τὰ ἅγια τοῖς ἁγίοις, *Sancta Sanctis*, "Holy things for holy persons." St. Cyril of Jerusalem thus explains and paraphrases the formula; "Holy are the gifts presented, since they have been visited by the Holy Ghost [in response to the Invocation]; holy are you also, having been vouchsafed the Holy Ghost [in Confirmation]; the Holy Things therefore correspond to holy persons." *

This proclamation is answered by the people in various forms, all breathing worship to our Lord Jesus Christ, and acknowledging Him, with the Father and the Spirit, as alone the Holy One. For instance, in the common Greek Liturgy (St. Chrysostom's) they say, "One is holy, One is the Lord, Jesus Christ, to the glory of God the Father." Or in the Clementine form, which embodies at this point the Angels' Song, as well as the Hosanna, which ordinarily followed the *Tersanctus:* "One is holy, One is the Lord, Jesus Christ, to the glory of God the Father, blessed forever. Amen. Glory to God in the highest, and on earth peace, good-will towards men. Ho-

---

* St. Cyril's Catechetical Lectures, translated in the Library of the Fathers, Lecture XXIII., p. 278. It should be needless to state that at a point much earlier in the service the unbaptized and the excommunicate had been dismissed from the Church.

sanna to the Son of David. Blessed is He Who cometh in the Name of the Lord; God, the Lord; and hath appeared to us. Hosanna in the highest." *

It should be noted that in the early Liturgies the worship paid to our Lord Jesus Christ at this point, as throughout the service, is distinctly not limited to His presence in the Sacrament. It is rather directed, as in our *Gloria in Excelsis*, to Him Who, while vouchsafing a special manifestation of His Presence in the Sacrament, " sitteth at the Right Hand of the Father." His Sacramental Presence is no coming down from His glory, no return to conditions of earthly limitation. It is rather because He is removed by the Ascension from all such limitations that He can manifest Himself, according to His good pleasure, and in ways of His appointment, at any and every time and place.

A prayer which in the Liturgies of St. Basil and St. Chrysostom, with a corresponding form in those called after St. Mark and St. James, immediately precedes the Elevation, may make this clear: " Give ear, O Lord Jesus Christ, our God, from Thy holy habitation, and from the

---

* For various responses to the *Sancta Sanctis*, see *Notitia Eucharistica*, pp. 597–600.

glorious throne of Thy kingdom, and come to sanctify us, Thou that sittest above with the Father, and art present invisibly with us here; and by Thy mighty hand vouchsafe to impart to us of Thy undefiled Body and precious Blood, and through us to all Thy people." *

3. The clause, "We praise Thee, we bless Thee, we worship Thee, we glorify Thee, we give thanks to Thee for Thy great glory," is with little doubt derived from the Liturgies named after St. Basil and St. Chrysostom, where a similar sentence of worship is sung by the choir between the recital of Our Lord's Words of Institution and the Invocation of the Holy Ghost: "We hymn Thee, we bless Thee, we give thanks to Thee, O Lord; and pray to Thee, our God."

There is an interesting addition to the hymn at this point in the Scottish Communion Service, which our American fathers did not adopt along with the Prayer of Consecration. Following, though not exactly, the version of the *Gloria*

---

* Hammond's *Liturgies*, pp. 121, 128; *Notitia Eucharistica*, pp. 850, 851; Introduction, p. xxvi.

This sort of Eucharistic Adoration, defended by Mr. Keble in his treatise on the subject (See especially pp. 57, 72, 141, 118) is plainly distinct from such practices as are connected with the Reservation of the Holy Sacrament for the purpose of Worship, *e.g.*, Benediction, Exposition, Visits to the Blessed Sacrament.

given in the Alexandrian manuscript of the Bible, the Scottish rite expands this doxology to include a distinct recognition of Each Person of the Blessed Trinity, adding after "O Lord God, heavenly King, God the Father Almighty" —"and to Thee, O God, the only begotten Son Jesu Christ; and to Thee, O God, the Holy Ghost." *

4. The insertion in the English Prayer-book of 1552 (and retained in ours) of the third address to the Lamb of God (the repetition of the clause, "Thou that takest away the sins of the world, have mercy upon us"), which is not found in any Greek or Latin copy of the hymn, if accidental in its origin, is remarkable as coinciding both with the change in the place of the hymn from the beginning to the end of the service, and with the omission from the prescribed service of the trine repetition of the *Agnus Dei* after the Prayer of Consecration. The insertion provides the familiar prayer, now embedded in the hymn, still after the Consecration, and in connection with the pleading of the Sacrifice.

The prayer we note is addressed to the Victorious Victim, the Lamb Who has been slain,

---

* See the interesting note in Bishop Dowden's *Annotated Scottish Communion Office.* (New York: Whittaker, 1884), pp. 223-231.

but Who stands triumphant before the throne, as One in inmost being and in glory with Him that sits upon the throne.* It calls on Him Who *now* " taketh away the sin of the world," and abolishes it, having in the Passion borne its burden and broken its power. To Him our exalted Saviour we cry to " receive our prayer," to " take away *our* sins," by the communication of His holiness, as we feed upon His Body and Blood, and are made thereby partakers of His Divine Nature, as He vouchsafed to partake of our human nature.

> " Behold the Lamb of God !
> Into the sacred flood
> Of Thy most precious blood
> My soul I cast !
> Wash me and make me clean within,
> And keep me pure from every sin,
> Till life be past." †

How could the Eucharistic Service better end than with this Hymn of mingled praise and prayer to Him that sitteth upon the throne and to the Lamb? We may, it seems to me, be thankful for the transposition of the *Gloria in Excelsis* from the opening of the service (where in its complete form it is hardly appropriate)

---

* Rev. v. 6, *sqq.*
† Matthew Bridges, in *The Hymnal*, No. 96.

to its close, where the hymn at once (1) gathers up the leading ideas of the whole rite; (2) serves as a thanksgiving for the gift we have received, such as was commonly found in the ancient Liturgies, the Roman herein departing from the general use;* and (3) may further remind us of the " hymn " which the Lord and the Apostles sang after the first Eucharist,† before going forth from the joyous and voluntary offering in the Upper Chamber to the sorrowful execution of that oblation in Gethsemane, at Gabbatha and Golgotha.‡ In glad remembrance of His redeeming struggle, we offer ourselves along with Him, our souls and bodies, a living sacrifice to God, and go forth from our Eucharistic worship to do all such good works as He has prepared for us to walk in, ready, after the example of our Lord and Elder Brother, to do and dare and bear all things for the Father's glory and the brethren's good.

"Glory to God in the highest, and on earth peace, good-will towards men."

---

* See Palmer's *Origines Liturgicæ*, Vol. II., pp. 157, 158; Scudamore, p. 690.

† St. Matthew xxvi. 30. Probably "the great Hallel," Pss. cxiii.-cxviii. See Meditation XLVII. in Fr. Benson's *Final Passover*, Vol. II., Part I.

‡ See Bishop Andrewes's *Devotions*, "An Act of Thanksgiving."

Hymns of the Daily Offices.

LECTURE III.

THE RT. REV. JOHN HAZEN WHITE, D.D.,
Bishop of Indiana.

HYMNS OF THE DAILY OFFICES.

Let the word of Christ dwell in you richly in all wisdom; teaching and admonishing one another in psalms, and hymns, and spiritual songs, singing with grace in your hearts to the Lord.
—*Colossians iii. 16.*

> " Over his keys the musing organist,
>   Beginning doubtfully and far away,
>   First lets his fingers wander as they list,
>   And builds a bridge from Dreamland for his lay;
>   Then as the touch of his loved instrument
>   Gives hope and fervor, nearer draws his theme,
>   First guessed by faint auroreal flushes sent
>   Along the wavering vista of his dream."
>   —*Lowell's Vision of Sir Launfal.*

It is in somewhat of this spirit that we approach the study of the hymns of the Nativity which constitute the canticles of the daily offices. With a diffidence begotten of the sense that our theme is three simple hymns uttered centuries agone by three humble souls we approach our subject timidly and with an air of irresolution. As the bird circles about its perch, uncertain where to alight, and then, emboldened by the welcome that awaits it, drops to the first inviting twig, only to spring from branch to branch in joyous ecstasy of home, so is the soul led along from truth to truth, from glory to glory, until it finds itself in a wealth of divine treasure which measures the value of the works we are studying and the exalted purposes which they may be made to serve. Small and great, simple and grand are thus ever blended in the divine economy to serve the purposes of the great Author of being and life. Glory is hidden in a snow-flake, power in a drop of dew, majesty in the lily of the field, and God in the Virgin's womb.

And so, dropping unconsciously the tardy hesitancy and the uncertain movement of approach for the deeper inspiration of eager expectancy, we press on to the grander truths treasured here and seek to probe them to their farthest recesses and their fullest blessing. The glory and power of the ocean is not discovered in the silent surface shimmering under the rays of the sun, but in its vasty deep, in its myriad mysteries lying below, in its hidden power released by a breath from heaven. So, too, under the finer analysis of spiritual discernment, the hymns of the Nativity, with all their simplicity, and devoid of that wealth of adornment which characterizes the poetry of the East, find their grandeur in the deep truths and mighty power hidden below. As of the great Master, to whose honor they owe their origin, of them it may in measure be said: " He has no form or comeliness; and when we shall see him, there is no beauty that we should desire him." As the sequence I trust may warrant, I have no hesitation in speaking of them as beautiful hymns. In speaking of these three beautiful hymns I shall touch first the circumstances of their origin, then on their bearing on the more august truths of prophecy, inspiration, divine worship, and the growth of the divine life in man; for so it is as we linger lovingly on the simple events that cluster about the coming of our dear Lord in human form, there steals in upon the soul the consciousness that mighty forces are at work here, designed to dismantle the bulwarks of sin, Satan, and death, and build the temple of eternity and the kingdom of light, and we are swept on into the contemplation of the mind of God and the modes of His operation and comprehension with which the events of time and eternity are enclosed in a word, as the deep in the hollow of His hand; swept on in thought, I say, until we begin to realize that these simple hymns hold in their utterances in perfect harmony the intricate history of God's dealings past, the tenderness and mercy of God's kingdom future, which resolve inspiration and prophecy of all their difficulties, invest divine worship with all its glory and power, and enrich human nature with all its grace and refinement under the magic influence of that holy term, sanctification; "This is the will of God, even your sanctification."

Let your minds dwell for a short period on the origin of these three hymns; how closely knit together they are in point of time, how harmonious in expression, what a unity of purpose marks their utterance, and yet how perfectly independent of each other. Zacharias, the doubting priest, yet intimately familiar through his daily vocation with the oracles of God, his mind stored with all the vivid forecasts of coming Messiah, had spent the time of his enforced suspension in dumb contemplation of the majesty and mercy of God. "It was all most fitting. The question of unbelief had struck the priest dumb, for most truly unbelief could not speak, and the answer of faith restored to him speech, for most truly doth faith loose the tongue. The first evidence of his dumbness had been that his tongue refused to speak the benediction, and the first evidence of his restored power was that he spake the benediction of God in a rapturous burst of praise and thanksgiving. The sign of the unbelieving priest standing before the awe-struck people vainly essaying to make himself understood by signs was most fitting; most fitting also that when they made signs to him what the new-born child should be called he burst in their hearing into a prophetic hymn:" *

Blessed be the Lord God of Israel; for he hath visited and redeemed his people,
And hath raised up a mighty salvation for us in the house of his servant David;
As he spake by the mouth of his holy Prophets, which have been since the world began;
That we should be saved from our enemies, and from the hand of all that hate us;
To perform the mercy promised to our forefather, and to remember his holy covenant;
To perform the oath which he sware to our forefather Abraham, that he would give us,
That we, being delivered out of the hand of our enemies, might serve him without fear,
In holiness and righteousness before him, all the days of our life.

---

* Edersheim's Life of Christ, Vol. I.

And thou, child, shalt be called the prophet of the Highest; for thou shalt go before the face of the Lord to prepare his ways;
To give knowledge of salvation unto his people, for the remission of their sins,
Through the tender mercy of our God; whereby the day-spring from on high hath visited us,
To give light to them that sit in darkness, and in the shadow of death, and to guide our feet into the way of peace.

Simple as is this outburst of praise, there is in it that which challenges not admiration alone, but holy awe. This is not human nature under its ordinarily expressed action, but human nature tempered, sublimated by some inner power, and lifted up to a height which human nature unaided never attained and never can attain. The consciousness of release from an affliction than which there can be none greater finds no recognition in the sublime utterances. The joyous sense of fatherhood, of escape from the unutterable loneliness of childlessness, is smothered under the jubilant emphasis of the fulfilled purposes of God to the human race. What a reaching back is there in these simple words over the centuries that were gone. What a gathering in of the ages to come. What an interpretation of promise, what an unfolding of prophecy, what a sweet and holy blending of the temporalities of Israel with the spiritualities of the kingdom of Christ, what a harmonizing of the mind of God with the life of man, what an overleaping of existing limitations in divine administration, even, what a comprehension of the brotherhood of the human race. Nor does the close connection that seems to exist between this beautiful hymn and the eighteen prayers of the temple service with which as a priest he was most familiar diminish aught from the awe with which we contemplate its first utterance, for it is characteristic of human nature under the sense of great personal benefit to sink all else in the joy with which it contemplates its latest blessing.

If we pass from the song of Zacharias to that of the Blessed Virgin, we shall meet even greater difficulty in reconciling the sweet, simple, and yet sublime utterances with conditions of human nature under which they were uttered. What human heart is capable of fathoming the conflicting emotions struggling for mastery in the soul of the betrothed maiden under the signal honor which had been bestowed upon her and the equally trying ordeal to which it exposed her ? To herself alone was known the message of the angel. To her espoused huband and to the world must soon be known her approaching motherhood. There is a tender touch of human nature in the narrative that almost immediately she sought the seclusion and privacy of the hill country, and the companionship of one who could share her knowledge and sympathize with her hopes and fears. Who can correctly picture her astonishment as she hears the salutation of her kinswoman, or suspect her of having prepared an answer of such sublimity as is presented in the Magnificat ? When we reflect that, while the angel had conveyed to the Blessed Virgin the tidings of her kinswoman's honor, no intimation had been imparted to Elizabeth that a higher honor should come to her home than the birth of her distinguished son, her salutation to her cousin invests itself with deeper mystery and dignity unsurpassed. "To be more precise, the words which filled with the Holy Ghost she spake were the mother's utterance to the mother, of the homage which her unborn babe offered to her Lord, while the answering hymn of Mary was the offering of that homage unto God. It was the antiphonal morning psalmody of the Messianic day as it broke, of which the words were of the old dispensation, but the music of the new." * If it were possible to suspect that the song of Zacharias was no more than the happy

---

* Edersheim's Life of Christ, Vol. I.

blending of ideas with which the learned priest had been long familiar through the recitation of his daily offices, all suspicion of such origin must fade away in the case of this simple maiden overpowered by her condition and confronted by such an unexpected and startling salutation. But there is no confusion, no embarrassment, no anxiety, no fear here. Serenity rules her heart, confidence her attitude, and trust her utterance; not feigned, but real. Again it is the glory of God, His faithfulness, His fulfilment, His mercy, His might, His far-reaching kingdom of reconciliation and peace. "When Isaac Newton saw an apple fall from a tree and asked himself the question why it did not go upwards instead of downwards, he had discovered the great law which governs the movements of the heavenly bodies, and when Mary surveyed her own history closely she recognized the universal principles of God's government in the world," * but here again her expression of this far exceeds the grasp of an ordinary human mind, and again this single note attracts to itself the unison of God's dispensation in the ages. Again there is no trace of the personal, the selfish, the narrow, the human. All this is

---

* Liddon's III Lecture on the Magnificat.

refined into obscurity, and there remains only the rapture of exultation in the universal, the divine, the permanent, and the triumphant.

My soul doth magnify the Lord, and my spirit hath rejoiced in God my Saviour.
For he hath regarded the lowliness of his handmaiden.
For behold, from henceforth all generations shall call me blessed.
For he that is mighty hath magnified me ; and holy is his Name.
And his mercy is on them that fear him throughout all generations.
He hath showed strength with his arm : he hath scattered the proud in the imagination of their hearts.
He hath put down the mighty from their seat, and hath exalted the humble and meek.
He hath filled the hungry with good things ; and the rich he hath sent empty away.
He remembering his mercy hath holpen his servant Israel ; as he promised to our forefathers, Abraham and his seed, forever.

The sequence of events and the sequence of prophetic hymns are together completed at the presentation of the Incarnate One in the temple. It is not without significance surely that this last beautiful song fell from the lips of one not connected by family with him who stands for the fall and rising again of many in Israel, but stands as a type of that vast company, who, filled with holy meditation, wait in hungry expectation for the day of the Lord, and of whom it may be said, " He longed to see my day and he saw it and was glad." That every age has such cannot be doubted. That God graciously, for the comfort of the faithful, found one such and conveyed to his hungry soul the blessed assurance that he should not see death till he had seen the Lord's Christ, is a mark of divine graciousness expressive of the minuteness of that provision which God has made for the completeness of his work. Still, if Elizabeth's salutation fell with startling surprise upon the ears of her lowly kinswoman, much greater must have been the surprise to both, as in the midst of the temple service the aged worshipper and the humble mother, with her offering permitted to poverty, come together, and taking the babe in his arms, Simeon has wrung from him as by constraint of the Holy Ghost alone, the words of his sweet prophecy, which of all others have endeared themselves to human hearts as the battle draws to a close and the sum of life's fluctuating aspirations crystalizes in the single beatitude of possessing God.

"With this infant in his arms it was as if he stood on the mountain height of prophetic vision and watched the golden beams of sunrise far away over the Isles of the Gentiles and then gathering their full glow over his beloved land and people. There was nothing Judaic, quite the contrary, only what was of the old Testament in what he first said." *

Lord, now lettest thou thy servant depart in peace, according to thy word :
For mine eyes have seen thy salvation,
Which thou hast prepared before the face of all people ;
To be a light to lighten the Gentiles, and to be the glory of thy people, Israel.

While there was for the aged Simeon no self-forgetfulness necessary in order to rise to his majestic prophecy, neither was there anything to prompt its expression. While there was the same comprehension of the far-reaching purposes of God which brought his hymn into perfect harmony with the other two and rendered them virtually one, is it too much to say, that the human race in the person of this aged and devout representative, yielded its prompt response of praise under the first conscious touch of the eternal blessing to rest upon it forever and flowing from the life of its Incarnate Lord?

With these holy hymns before us, illumined by the events that gave them birth, we are prepared for their deeper study. Almost instantly and instinctively we recognize that they draw away from all human songs, and align themselves

---

* Edersheim's Life of Christ, Vol. I.

with those of Moses and Miriam, Hannah and Deborah in the older dispensation, and that song of Moses and the Lamb which in anticipation we hear resounding through the courts of heaven, the unison of the multitudinous host of the redeemed; and almost as readily do we detect that they far excel all others of their own class in the reach of their vision, and the delicacy and accuracy of their interpretation of the mind of God, reducing to a common purpose the history of the past and the more gracious dispensation of the future, as the great Apostle puts it when he says, "According to the eternal purpose which he purposed in Christ Jesus."

If these beautiful songs are marked by an absence of all themes that ordinarily move the human soul to song, and all form in which the soul so moved gives expression to the conscious emotion within it; if they rise to grander heights and touch with greater tenderness the as yet undeveloped glories of which human nature is capable, the secret of their isolated and yet common distinction is to be found alone in the close contact with the Incarnate God. It is a mistake to conceive of these beautiful songs as the natural productions of human minds, however gifted. They are no carefully thought-out, elaborately embellished productions of the library. They reflect none of the inquisitive human study into the mysteries of nature, none of the triumphs of human effort over the obstacles to human hope, which prompt the songs of common, but gifted, singers. They are the spontaneous, unpremeditated outbursts of spiritual song under the deep impulse imparted to those who uttered them by the touch of the Incarnate Life. They represent, if they represent anything at all, the first touch of the Incarnation and its effect upon the human soul and human mind, presaging and forecasting all that glorious refinement of human nature, equipping it for a service more glorious than the tilling of fields or waging of wars, which it was the final purpose of the Incarnation to develop by the diffusion of its power and purpose. Ignorance, weakness, humility, self-interest, are as nothing under the potency of this persistent influence. The light of the world disinfects it of the seeds of disease and death, and imparts to it the capacity for expansion, ascension, new forms, new service. Natural endowments, with all their natural limitations, are as nothing under the touch of the Incarnate Life. A new capacity is imparted to them, a new inspiration, a new impulse, a new possibility, and with it a new expression of hope and joy in the fulfilment of hope. That is the great purpose of the Incarnation, to impart to the natural man, mentally, spiritually, yes, and physically, too, when we consider the great truth of the resurrection of the body, that which by nature he cannot have. As the sun steals over the horizon and his first rays touch and gild the ragged mountain peaks, hitherto obscured in darkness, each separate shaft shoots out in clear outline, and between lie the dark caverns to be penetrated by the later rays of the fuller orb; or as he sends his subtle shaft to the root of plant and flower, the vital fluid springs through tingling veins to hungry buds that wait its coming. Buds burst, blossoms blow, new life reigns everywhere. So under the touch of that divine communication flowing through the Incarnate Life to half-developed human souls, nature is mollified, relaxes its stern tension, surrenders its severe indifference, forgets its anxious selfishness, yields to the gladness of higher inspiration, abandons itself to the glorification of God, enters with vivid sympathy into His holy and eternal purposes, realizing the burden of its earlier bondage and the dignity with which God hath made us free. No fact is perhaps so widely confessed and practically so forgotten as God's action on the affairs of the world and of men's separate lives. Dew and rain are natural and necessary forces in human estimation; "He bloweth with His wind and the waters flow," but that He lifteth up or casteth down is inconceivable when applied to the multitude of men. The sea may yield to His impulse, but the human soul cannot be affected by His purpose and His power. The Holy Ghost and His operations must be invested with unreality or suspected of impotence. The natural effect of distinction of whatever sort is to fill the soul with conscious superiority and pride and prepare it to receive adulation and praise. The touch of God is designed to efface all this, and impart in its stead humility, dependence, obedience, realizing the purpose of the gift, and rendering merited praise to the Giver in His holy presence. It is this transforming, transfusing, glorifying influence which is apparent in the three lives we are studying and the expression it received in the hymns of the Nativity.

And again permitting ourselves to be deflected from the immediate line of our study, we are carried on to the contemplation of those two intricate truths, prophecy and inspiration, which play so prominent a part in the evolution of the great mystery of Godliness, and carry in themselves that evidence of God's mysterious handiwork. For prophecy and inspiration, in all that they imply, are closely and intimately intertwined in these songs of the Nativity; prophecy, the conveyance to the human soul of knowledge yet hidden with God, but to be worked out by God in obedience to His unchangeable purpose; and inspiration, the guidance of the human mind in giving expression to that knowledge and interpretation to divine purpose in such wise as to secure the eternity of truth and harmony of plan to all God's working. In all of these songs of the Nativity there is mingled to a marked and most positive degree both prophecy and inspiration as they touched the person of the Christ, gave character to His dispensation, intimation of the scope of its operations, or suggestion of the deeper element in human nature designed to be enriched, glorified, prepared for receiving the further favor of God, the gift of eternal life, and for which provision was made of God in the Incarnation. The human mind through its philosophizings has built up enormous artificial obstacles to lie between itself and God and obstruct and delay its entrance into that rich inheritance, which eye hath not seen, nor ear heard, nor the mind of man conceived of, which God hath prepared for them that with undivided loyalty love Him.

Nothing can be more shallow and void of wisdom than the limitations which the human mind would impose upon divine power in expressing itself through these two sacred systems employed of God for conducting the human soul from darkness to light, from ignorance of all things to knowledge of God, the author of all. For consider, first of all, that all truth is but an emanation from the mind of God, and expresses that which from all eternity has reposed in the mind of God, including all that has the capacity of endurance, and excluding all that is perishable because opposed to the mind of God; and then that all existence and all operation is but a conveyance from God of that truth which was forever in the mind of God to creatures of His own planning and capable of receiving it, containing it, and exhibiting it to Himself or to lower orders of intelligence which were invested with something of His own capacity for knowledge. Truth as it is in matter, truth as it is in force, is but a conveyance to a lower order of creatures of that mysterious existence which lies wrapped in their being; but the human soul, with its capacity for knowledge, represents nothing else than the highest order of God's creatures, to which He has conveyed a gift vouchsafed to none other than it, that of sharing the knowledge possessed by Himself. But shall it be said that God has limited this higher order of His creatures in its acquisition of knowledge to its labored interpretation of this lower order to which God has conveyed some portion of His truth, and that He who has conveyed what of truth lies hidden in a drop of dew or in the wandering winds or the shifting sea cannot convey the same truth to the human soul save through the instrumentality of a voiceless and soulless material existence; or that God cannot and shall not convey to the human soul the knowledge of such truth until such time as it shall have been first conveyed to some lower order of creatures and through them be made operative in the realms of nature or history. I am touching here a very deep truth, demanding close thought for its interpretation. I affirm that the same creator that can convey to heat the power to expand metals, and to the human intelligence the capacity to understand that fact through its operation, can convey that knowledge to the human intelligence independent of its operation if He sees fit to do so. The conveyance to the human soul directly of the knowledge of the Incarnation even is not more marvellous than the conveyance of the same knowledge to the human soul through the Incarnation as a fact. The transforming of water into wine through the ordinary process of the growth of the grape, the expressing of its juices, and the process of fermentation carries knowledge to the observing and reflecting mind of man. The power which conveyed this capacity to the grape can convey the knowledge of it to the intelligent creature man without the help of unintelligent matter.

But let us proceed to a higher aspect of the same great truth, the capacity of the vessel to contain, hold, and express truth as it is in the mind and purpose of God without understanding it. It is sometimes considered an objection to prophecy and inspiration that the human agencies through which they were expressed had no just sense of the significance of the service they were rendering, and that to later ages was reserved the privilege of discovering the deep truths unfolded by these messengers of long ago. Grant all this, and it but expresses a universal principle of existence. It is incontestably true that matter contains in its keeping and is constantly expressing profound truth which it does not and can never understand, because it is devoid of any intelligent faculty. The earth has no understanding of the power of gravitation, yet it holds it in its being, exercises it, and is regulated by it. The understanding, then, of the mighty gifts of God and the power which they exercise and the purpose which they are to serve is not essential to their true reception and operation. Nor does the human soul, with all its intelligent capacity, differ materially in any respect from inanimate life in this regard. It has intrusted to its keeping and exercise enormous powers and splendid truths which through ages past it did not understand and which to-day it but faintly comprehends. Light, heat, and electricity have with subtle influences been playing about us from the first, and yet the human understanding is but beginning to resolve them of their secrets. The spiritual nature of man has all along been subject to the influences that cast it down and lift it up, depress it with fear and inspire it with hope, yet imperfect still is the human understanding of the agency which produces the one or the other. I desire to emphasize most forcibly that the understanding of the truths of creation, redemption, sanctification, of matter and spirit, of nature and grace, are not essential to their existence; more than this, to affirm that the understanding of the wonderful works of God is reserved to remote ages, to eternity, while every age is privileged to possess and profit by that work. "Brethren, now are we the sons of God, and it doth not yet appear what we shall be, but we know that when He shall appear we shall be like Him, for we shall see Him as He is."

Or, to take another aspect of this great subject. Must the employment of the human soul as an agency for prophecy or inspiration impair, efface, or entirely destroy the natural gifts of the agent so employed? Or to put it more clearly, are we to question the truth and accuracy of God's operation in the kingdom of grace because we discover that the agents so employed retain without impairment the other gifts, which, as we say, by nature they have received? All nature revolts against such an inference. The physical nature of man does not lose its peculiar characteristics by reason of the solids, liquids, and gases which pass through its various organs. Matter retains its distinctive attributes although the vehicle of forces fitted to operate through its agency. The air we breathe is not bereft of its potency though a convenient medium of sound. Is all this to be lost upon human intelligence as it comes to the study of God's kingdom of grace? Must prophecy and inspiration be resolved into no more than the natural expression of the natural man with all the limitations which the existing state of human knowledge imposed simply because the natural man still continued to exhibit the evidence that he was man and had not been transformed into God? In all this I affirm that we are brought face to face with the purpose of the Incarnation, which was to impart to man that which by nature he cannot have. That it did impart to nature that which by nature it did not have is the basic truth of Christian hope, Christian faith, Christian life. Sweet, simple, beautiful are the songs of the Nativity; grand do they become in their evidential value as witnessing to the power which God conveyed to humble and simple souls to interpret mysteriously the history of the past and unfold accurately the character and operation of that marvellous dispensation then ushered in and destined to exert a more potent influence upon human souls than the visible works of nature and the powers hidden within them, types and figures of the things which are not seen but are eternal.

And so our study of these songs of the Nativity carries us irresistibly to the conclusion that they are not mere productions of the natural man, and irresistibly to the conclusion that they owe their being to their contact with the Incarnate life, carries us to the further thought that the power which inspired their production has governed their use.

That the touch of the Incarnate Life operated to the production of songs so intensely sublime, in which were mingled exquisitely spiritual interpretations of events past, and distinct intimations of future aspects of Christ's influence on the world, suggests at once the further purpose underlying their production than their relation to those by whom they were uttered; that they were preserved to posterity, and that through the agency of the Holy Spirit is more than suggestive that posterity was to derive a benefit from them commensurate with the care bestowed upon their production and preservation.

Not to miss the full significance of the liturgical use of these songs of the Nativity, it becomes us to mark how universal has been their employment in public worship in all branches of the

Church from the first until now. To that end we must consider carefully what the Church is, and how it has preserved a true conception of public worship from age to age, and been divinely guided to make employment of such provisions for public worship as to preserve all the essential elements of public worship as acceptable to the mind of God.

The consciousness that the Incarnate Life was designed to affect and benefit all life to remotest ages prepares us to follow the stages by which it has affected human life and imparted to it its virtues. Among the notable results of the Incarnation is the direction of the Church into a true, healthful order of public worship, and the preservation of the same through all the mutations of the ages. The transition is not difficult from the natural body of Christ to the mystical body, the Church, and the Church becomes the natural body expanded by that close union which knits to it every individual incorporated into it by an ingrafting so actual and effectual as to render it a participant in all the virtues, powers, capacities imparted to it by reason of the Incarnation. It has been beautifully said that the Sacraments are the expansion of the Incarnation, so that through them the Church becomes the body in which Christ dwells. Christ's sacraments produce their effects not after the manner of a holy charm in virtue merely of His promise to them, but as causes by reason of His presence in them. It has been well observed that the Church's rites, even of her most ordinary ones, are based upon the deepest doctrinal mysteries. If this be true, we are to find our interpretation of the Church's acts in the solemn mystery of Christ's dwelling in her, and as closely imparting to her movements, as to His natural body, the impress of His will and holy purpose. The acts of the Church become then as the acts of Zacharias, the Blessed Virgin, and Simeon, something more than the expression of human judgment and taste, the channels for the effectual fulfilment of the mind of God. The Catholic Church then represents something more than the continuity of organization. The Catholic Church is simply one department in that great executive realm in which God is King and divine power the operating agent. The unchangeableness of God is the surety for the unchangeableness of the kingdom in which the mind and power of God are expressed so far as they relate to the spirit world. Just here we are brought face to face with two aspects of Christ's life, and if of Christ's life, then of the Church's mission as affected by Christ's indwelling presence. " There are, as it would seem, two special mysteries of the Christion religion, in the right understanding of the one or the other of which, or of both taken together, we may find the answer to most questions concerning either ritual or practice which can rise under that dispensation. These are the Incarnation and the Priesthood of Christ. In these two facts, taking both of them in their widest sense, is summed up the whole of our Lord's operations in behalf of His Church. The Priesthood of Christ, though most closely and intimately connected with His Incarnation, yet seems capable of being discriminated from it as a second and distinct step in His great work. The Incarnation was in order to the Priesthood, but did not properly involve it. Christ's Body was prepared Him in order that, like all other Priests, He might have somewhat to offer. The action of His Priesthood supervened upon the proper action of His Incarnation. What He was as man He offered as Priest. The obedient sonship was sanctified and offered in the office of the Eternal Priesthood." *

---

* Freeman's Principles of Divine Service, Vol. II.

It seems most natural, then, to find these two aspects of the Incarnate Life passing from it to the Church, His body, and through it expressing themselves in its visible life. As touching human life with which it came in contact, quickening, reviving, purifying, hallowing, and sanctifying it, but carrying it on and presenting the body so sanctified as an acceptable oblation to God.

Besides the restoration of man to the image of God, the divine purpose included the setting on foot of certain new and bettered relations to Himself on the part of the creature so restored. Now all this carries with it the idea of public worship as one of the main purposes of the Incarnation, to be reproduced and regulated by the indwelling of Christ; the bringing of mankind from its dismembered condition into a single body, the bringing of that body into the presence of God, into communion and fellowship with God subserviently to those true conceptions of God which alone admit of man entering His presence or addressing to Him prayer or praise.

As thus considered, divine worship becomes something far different from an imperfectly defined impulse of emotion, variable with the taste and knowledge of the offerer, now violently effusive, now devoid of all connection with the operation of the Holy Spirit, and now characterized by the vapid utterances of an excited intellect. Divine worship, as historically considered, represents the indwelling of the Holy Spirit, drawing man into God's presence under the conscious influence of all the conditions under which entrance into God's presence may with safety and benefit be made. The Church therefore presents to us throughout her history not merely a divine agency exercising her powers manward, teaching, reproving, rebuking, admonishing, and feeding, but in the same holy influence approaching God with a glorified service, in which are mingled purifyings, penitences, praises, thanksgivings, rejoicings, and blessings; and through all her history the Church seems to have been divinely guided to find her material for public worship in the vehicles divinely provided for that end.

These vehicles have kept clearly in view all along that sin and self-will effectually and forever exclude from God's presence, and that admission to Him rests solely upon regeneration, restoration to His image, conformity to His will. The efficacious instruments of His mercy then become the objects of solicitude and the themes of praise. The value of all this can only be realized when we justly compare the results of public worship under its historic guidance and the state to which it has been reduced by human direction independent of the impulse of the Incarnate Life. In this connection I am constrained to quote at some length the words employed by Hallam in his first lecture on Morning Prayer. On the one hand, he says, all features of public worship unite to exhibit a particular aspect of God and a particular aspect of man, and this aspect may be called the evangelical as contradistinguished from the rationalistic on the one hand and from the enthusiastic on the other. It exhibits God as a holy being and an upright ruler, hating sin and punishing transgressors, yet extending favor to contrite offenders through a system of mercy which at once vindicates His holiness and rectitude and confers pardon and acceptance on all those who confess their sins and forsake them. It exhibits man as sinful and guilty, condemned by the law of God and justly subject to His displeasure, but encouraged by the promises and offers of God's love to hope and seek for forgiveness and restoration, in the exercise of a hearty repentance and true faith. It proclaims this the worship of a holy, just, but merciful and forgiving God by humble and penitent sinners. Let no self-righteous Pharisee, whether he be a proud votary of reason or a bold, presumptuous enthusiast enter here. It distinctly defines the position of our worship, placing it between the desert, frozen with perpetual frost of that school which calls itself rational, and that other desert, parched with irregular and wasting fires of heated and disorderly enthusiasm, which border it on either side, and fencing it from both with precision and security. On the one side we see a worship that is essentially rationalistic, out of which all that is truly characteristic and distinctive of the real Gospel of Christ has been stealthily withdrawn, leaving but the empty shell or carcass, without the substance or the life. This is the very soil out of which grow what may be called fancy prayers, eloquent and poetic apostrophes and appeals to the great, all-pervading, all-doing Spirit Unseen. Nature becomes one great inexhaustible magazine to finish out the wardrobe of this sentimental worship. In the hands of an intelligent and refined operator prayer may be wrought up in this way into a very charming performance, as an artistic production very beautiful, very touching, very agreeable and engaging, while in the hands of the less gifted and skilful it descends into a piece of mawkish and vapid sentimentality. But in the one variety and the other alike, to the soul that hungers and thirsts after righteousness it is utterly empty and unsatisfying. Such talk to an earnest soul is a mere mockery and disappointment. You could as soon satisfy a craving appetite with wind, or fatten a hungry man with ashes. The poetry of devotion is not a thing on which the human soul can live. Coming with the burdens of real wants to a real God, it craves the language of reality, it seeks directness and conciseness. The true beauty of prayer is the beauty of fitness and propriety, the true eloquence of prayer the apt and weighty words wrung out by the urgency of need and desire. Who ever heard of a prisoner pleading for his life with the flowers of rhetoric? Save, Lord, or I perish— that is prayer, eloquent, beautiful prayer. But rationalism employs the treasures of science and the moving panorama of human life to furnish out pictures of which it cannot be slanderous to say they are addressed to the fancies and sensibilities of men and not to the great and fatherly heart of the glorious God. On the other hand,

and scarcely less to be avoided, is what I have called a worship of enthusiasm, in which the true relations of God and man are in a different way, but hardly less fatally, misrepresented and obscured. This is the region of fervid confidence, in which God and man are placed in relations to each other essentially just; but the one is lowered from the lofty place He rightly fills, and the other elevated equally above his true position. All this arises from the admixture of animal excitement and sensibility with the true operation of saving grace; and this is the legitimate result of popular notions of its nature and the methods of seeking and cherishing its influences. The result is a sensuous religion, not fed, as in the Church of Rome, by crucifixes and images and pictures, and expending itself in telling beads and genuflections, but living just as sensuously in noise and vehemence and boisterousness, in familiarity and colloquialism of speech, on the whole, in such a forgetfulness of the wide and awful distance between the forgiven sinner and the holy God, and of the vast work yet to be done in the renewed heart before it reaches any near approximation to the true standard of holiness as is fatal to all true reverence and all really devout and solemn worship.

The adoption of sons under this delusion is vindicated in freedoms which a well-nurtured earthly sonship would scruple to use; and love finds vent in terms of endearment replete with the lusciousness of an ill-trained physical affection. And thus the height of spirituality is thought to be attained in a sort of religious intoxication, under which the soul revels in an utter abandonment of restraint and sobriety. Where such notions of religion prevail, worship becomes either a straining after this exalted state of feeling, or an indulgence of it in the free outpouring of extravagence and excitement, or the assumed appearance of it, as essential to an authentic and acceptable exercise of devotion.

But the worship which the mind of God has fashioned for the healthful service of man is temperate in all things. The confidence of a certain faith, the comfort of a reasonable, religious, and holy hope it has, but it has no confidence in the virtues of nature nor in the transports of grace. It is calm, serene, still, distrustful of itself and of the world, keeping its way through life in Godly quietness, leaning only on the hope of God's heavenly grace and looking for the mercy of our Lord Jesus Christ unto eternal life.

It is not a fact to be lightly regarded that the

Church has universally and with a unanimity that is deeply impressive refrained from what is called extemporary and humanly devised forms of worship, but has as uniformly made use of the inspired writings for her acts of worship, whether jubilant or mournful, penitential or Eucharistic. There is a touch of deep solemnity in the earnestness with which both the Jewish and Christian Churches have made use of the songs of Moses, of Hannah, Habbakuk, and Hezekiah, and the Psalms for all their devotions, only imparting to them a spiritual significance, as on the morning of the resurrection they sing the song of Moses at the Red Sea. We are now prepared to understand what without it would be most mysterious, the uniformity with which the Church has from the beginning made use of the Benedictus, the Magnificat, and the Nunc Dimittis in her public offices. I need not dwell here upon the spread of the Church throughout the world, one, and yet appearing as national churches with varying offices of public worship, nor rehearse how the early ordinary offices arranged themselves as Nocturns, Lauds, Matins, Prime, Terce, Sext, Nones, Vespers, and Compline. What I desire most is to emphasize the fact that all, as by a common consent, as moved by a single impulse, made use of these three songs of the Nativity as expressing the conscious reception of the benefits of the Incarnation, and as expressing the joy incident thereto in language the most fitting as itself framed by the Holy Ghost Himself. And thus, as by a true spirit of interpretation, the Benedictus came to connect itself with Lauds, the Magnificat with Vespers, and the Nunc Dimittis with Compline. In that later revision of the offices of the Church whereby these were gathered into two offices, one for Matins, the other for Vespers, and lections were introduced, that there might be knowledge and apprehension of Him by the understanding, the will, and the affections, these venerable canticles, preserved and transmitted to posterity, serve, as they should, as the responsories to the teachings which bring to the soul the Incarnation, with all its benefits and blessings, through the lessons of Holy Scripture. It is ever thus that the two aspects of the Christ Life, the Incarnation and the Priesthood, work their benefits upon human souls, and by the same instruments first preparing us, body, soul, and spirit, for presentation to God, and then enabling us to present ourselves acceptably to Him. But if it be objected that this is artificially done, let us grant that it is so; but it is divine art. In her offices of public worship the Church has ever made use of all the resources at her command to awaken in man's inner self a just sense of his relation to God, a painful sense of the enormity of sin, and the equally appalling thought of the divine remedy for it. By all the devices known to her, by all the treasures provided for her of God, the Church seeks to bring mankind into a genuine state of pain, sorrow, remorse, tears, weeping, mourning, which shall issue in renunciation of evil, in the acceptance of Christ as Saviour, Master, King, and to the expression in fitting terms to God of the transformation thus wrought within it by the Incarnate Life conveyed to it. But because all this is artificial is it unprofitable? All art is but the application of divinely appointed means to divinely intended ends. Tired with the work of life, we realize our need of pleasure. Are not all our devices for rousing the weary, depressed soul, and imparting to it the invigorating joyousness that makes labor light, artificial? Or, to take another illustration, is not the State most assiduous in her care to cultivate patriotism, making use of art, literature, eloquence, and every fitting occasion or historical anniversary for bringing this into her service? Shall the children of this world be wiser in their generation than the children of light? The Church's holy seasons are artificially observed. Her devices are of Christ's planning. She is charged to diligence and constancy in their use for the very reason that daily contact with the world tends to destroy that very state of the soul which is essentially necessary to the cultivation and preservation of holiness in all its parts. Artificially the Church seeks to counteract this effect produced upon mind and soul by the world and the world's work, but it is divine art.

" May we not reverently express the hope that the day is far distant when the Church shall exchange this venerable order of public worship with all the venerated associations connected with it for the poverty of improvised and emotional individualism or the solitary isolation of the daily Mass?

" In our country alone, in one form alone, does the western, the ancient western, office survive —psalmody, scripture, responsive canticles, preces, collects, the medium of Europe's ancient worship, banished from all other lands, have taken refuge in the Churches of the English Communion. The English Church is in this matter the heir of the world. She may have diminished her inheritance, but all other western churches have thrown it away. The question is between these ordinary offices or none." * God grant her grace to sacredly preserve them, diligently use them, and devoutly love them, to His glory and her profit. Amen.

---

* Freeman's Principles of Divine Service, Vol. II.

The Hymns of the Ordinal.

LECTURE IV.

THE RT. REV. HENRY C. POTTER, D.D., LL.D., D.C.L.,
Bishop of New York.

THE HYMNS OF THE ORDINAL.

As human society passes out of its more primitive into its more complex forms, it illustrates, whatever may be its lesser diversities, two general modes or forms of expression which are indicative of two enduring tendencies in human nature. One of these is in the direction of individual freedom, and finds its manifestation in those matters of personal conduct which cannot be said to follow any fixed law. A despotism may erect, above the people that it rules, a vast and intricate mechanism of precept and prohibition; but the individual will somehow find, even within the narrow restrictions of its most rigorous limitations—as the handcuffed prisoner still moves his fingers and signals thus, it may be, to his fellow-prisoner—some mode of action and of expression. At the basis of human consciousness lies the freedom of the human will, and, with it, all the impatience of the manifold forms of bondage to law, and limitation of individual action, for which that instinct stands.

And, over against that universal instinct there is disclosed, just as widely, precisely as society advances out of its simpler forms into those that are higher and more complex, another tendency or movement, and one ultimately more dominant, and this is the tendency to limit and qualify individual liberty and impulse by prescribed form and precept. Indeed, this development may be said to mark what may be called the secondary as distinguished from the primary period in all human association. By this road civilization comes. Under the operation of this tendency the pastoral state and community give place to one which limits the nomadic impulse, which fences round the individual life with rules and restraints; and which, developing in time what we call government develops with it those fixed forms, rules, ceremonials, oaths, symbols, official personages, and the rest, by means of which government is maintained and perpetuated.

All this, I say, is true of human society; and, if these brief moments allowed, it would be a very interesting process to trace those memorable and often picturesque steps by which it has come to pass. But I have brought you thus far by lines that may seem to you, so far as the subject set for this occasion is concerned, equally remote and obscure, simply that you may recognize that that which is true of human society is no less true of that other society not merely human but divine, which we call the Church of God. I am to speak to you of the Hymns of the Ordinal; I cannot, however, well do so without saying something, first of all, of the Ordinal itself. What is the Ordinal? How did it come to be? What relation have the other parts of it to those hymns of which we are to speak? We go back to the first pages in the story of the genesis of the Church and they tell us, some one may say, nothing of an Ordinal. The Divine Founder of the Christian Fellowship calls some twelve men or some seventy men, as the case may be, around Him and gives them their commission to teach, to preach, to baptize. He appears to them after His Resurrection, and breathes upon them, saying, "Receive ye the Holy Ghost; whose sins ye remit they are remitted unto them; and whose sins ye retain they are retained." Or again, the Apostles come together when there is a vacancy in their original number, and pray, saying, "Thou, Lord, which knowest the hearts of all men, show whether of these two (Joseph called Barsabas, or Matthias) thou hast chosen."* Or yet again, "The twelve called the multitude of the disciples together and said, Look ye out from among you seven men of honest report, full of the Holy Ghost and wisdom, whom we may appoint" as helpers in the work of the Church; and when, in obedience to this command, Stephen and the rest are chosen; then we read that these were "set before the Apostles, and when they had prayed, they laid their hands on them." † Or, still again we read, "The Holy Ghost said, Separate me Barnabas and Saul for the work whereunto I have called them. And when they had fasted and prayed, and laid their hands on them, they sent them away.‡ This, I say, we find in that volume which is the story of the beginnings of the Christian Church, and as we do so we say 'How simple it all is; how informal, how natural and instinctive!' Yes, doubtless, as was the whole of the life of the Church in those primitive and formative days of which these events were a part. But we look

---

* Acts i. 15 *et seq.* † Acts vi. 1–7. ‡ Acts xiii. 2, 3.

again, and then as we turn, for example, to those Offices which give to our Ordinal of to-day its distinctive name, I mean the Offices for the Ordering of Deacons and Priests, and for the Ordaining and Consecrating of Bishops, we see how close, after all, through all the changing centuries, to those primitive and scriptural models which I have quoted, these later Offices have clung.

Through all the changing centuries, I say. What was it, now, which it might obviously and reasonably be expected that these should bring to pass? First of all, it was to be expected that, with the growth of the Church, those offices by which men were set apart for any sacred function should take on such features as that growth itself compelled. The challenge to the people concerning the fitness of one about to be ordained would be unnecessary in a small and intimate fellowship. But, with greater numbers come greater perils from unfitness, unworthiness, unreflectingness; and so there may be traced in what may be called the evolution of the Offices of Ordination a marked development in those features which emphasize the due guards and requirements which are designed as guarantees of character, competency, and fitness.

Again: in the progress of the life of the Church it was to be expected that National Churches should develop in connection with all the offices of the common religion, such diversities as would be characteristic and distinctive of national traditions and peculiarities, oriental and occidental, highly civilized or less civilized, as in fact they did—as might be shown, did these limits permit it, in connection, *e.g.*, with the particular matter of the transmission of authority, as illustrated in the *form* of Ordination or Consecration. In the Alexandrian and Abyssinian Churches, *e.g.*, as the author of "Christian Institutes" has shown,* this "was and still is by breathing; in the Eastern Church, generally by lifting up the hands in the ancient oriental attitude of benediction; in the Armenian Church, as also at times in the Alexandrian, by the dead hand of the predecessor; in the early Celtic Church by the transmission of relics or the pastoral staff; in the Latin Church by the laying on of hands; to which may be added an oriental usage traceable to the time of the "Apostolic Constitutions" which required that an open copy of the Gospels should be laid upon the head or neck of the person to be ordained.

---

* Stanley's Christian Institutes, p. 212. Scribner's Ed.

THE HYMNS OF THE ORDINAL. 129

But all these diversities touched minor and insignificant things; and nothing is more impressive in a review of these forms by which, from earlier ages, the authority of Orders has been handed down, than the fact that there is to be found in all of them, as their central and supreme characteristic, the invocation of the Holy Spirit. In the Office for the Ordination of Deacons, as set forth in our own Book of Common Prayer and as obtaining in the Anglican Communion throughout the world, there is indeed, in the actual formula accompanying the laying on of hands nothing that answers to the elder formula of the Salisbury Use which enjoins the words " Accipe Spiritum Sanctum; " but there is a special petition in the Litany which reads " That it may please thee to bless these thy servants now to be admitted to the Order of Deacons and to pour thy grace upon them," and it may also be mentioned that the Pontifical of Salisbury, to which I have referred, was substantially identical, in its ordaining formula, with that of Bangor and other later Latin uses, as it was with that of very early Eastern usage still obtaining in the Greek Church.* And what is even more beautifully

---

* Morin, de Sacr. Ordin. Part I., p. 79, D.

significant is the fact that, in the Sacramentary of Gregory the Bishop, in the " Benedictio Diaconi," commends those who are to be ordained to the prayers of the people substantially in these words: " Let us, Beloved Brethren, pray the Omnipotent Father that upon these who are accounted worthy to assume the office of a Deacon He will mercifully pour down (or shed down, *effundat*) the grace of His benediction."

The truth which underlies all this is a fundamental one; and it is because so impressively they emphasize it that the Hymns, or Hymn, in the Ordinal (for, in fact, apart from the Eucharistic Hymns, which are a part of that office, and which, as such, are necessarily used in connection with an Ordination, since, according to the rubrical law of the Church, there can be no Ordination without a celebration of the Holy Communion, there is, as we shall presently see, but one Hymn)—it is, I say, because the Hymn in the Office for the Ordination of Priests or the Consecration of Bishops so impressively emphasizes that which is central to the office, that it stands just where it is. That without which the Service of Ordination would have no other than a merely secular meaning is its invocation of the Sevenfold gifts of the Holy Ghost.

The presentation by the Archdeacon or his representative, the challenge to the people, the petition of the Litany, the examination and pledges of the candidate, all these have their proper place in such an office, most of all, as leading up to that of which they are the portal. But that which most truly confers the grace of Orders is the sevenfold gift of the Holy Ghost. There are ceremonials in connection with Ordination which, since the Reformation settlement, have disappeared out of it, and some may think, perhaps, that those offices have lost not a little by their elimination. The question is not one which I shall attempt to discuss here, though I am quite free to say that if the true ideal in the Church's offices be, as a great authority in our mother Church has declared, " a certain stately simplicity," * those offices must be owned to have gained immensely by the disappearance of features often puerile, and oftener still fantastic. But be that as it may, the matter of supreme congratulation with us may well be that no changes have touched that which is central in the Office; the prayer for the gifts of the Holy Ghost, and the solemn invocation of those

---

* Mr. Beresford Hope.

gifts, accompanied by the laying on of hands. We go back to those Ordinals used in England in the fifth century and we find indisputable evidence of this essential fact. We trace the stream of testimony down through the Sacramentaries of St. Leo, Gelasius, Gregory, the *Liturgia Alemannica* (which belongs to the ninth century), the Gallican Liturgy, the Pontifical of Egbert, and so on, until we come to the well-defined Use of Salisbury, and the token of this consistent and dominant tradition is everywhere to be found. With the dawn of the English Reformation there came, of course, extensive changes, the first and most necessary of which was the casting out of the corrupt oath of obedience to the Bishop of Rome; and then, consistently with this, the elimination of those features to which I have already referred, no one of which had any slightest Scriptural or primitive warrant, and none of which was older than the eighth or ninth Century, eras in the history of the Catholic Church marked by gross ignorance and widespread superstition. These changes were made by a commission of Bishops and others appointed for that purpose, and the result of their labors we have to-day in the Forms, or Offices, contained in our own Book of Common Prayer.

Their general outlines I have already indicated, and it now remains to me to turn to that particular feature in them of which to-day I have been bidden to speak. In the Office for the Ordaining of a Priest and in that for Ordaining and Consecrating a Bishop there is introduced, immediately before the brief prayer which precedes the laying on of hands, a Hymn which, in the Ordinal, still bears the title that in that ancient tongue in which it was written was originally given to it, of " Veni Creator Spiritus."

No more interesting page can be found in Christian history than that on which the story of this Hymn is written. Indeed, if one were to trace it to its ultimate source it would demand not a page, but a volume. One takes up this single slender thread and straightway becomes conscious that its farther end lies not merely among the beginnings of Christianity itself, but beyond them. The place of the Hymn, in other words, in Christian worship, how it came there, what were the influences that bred and modified, what were the motives that craved and used it, these are undoubtedly inquiries that lie about the foundations of Christian Society in its earliest days and its most primitive forms. As the new Religion emerged out of the darkness of that elder paganism which had preceded it, it could not, for instance, forget that that Paganism had its own cult, its own worship, its own liturgical rites. The Greek convert, as he lingered near the Areopagus, heard the strains in which Hesiod sang to Zeus, or hymned "the glories of men of old and the gods of Olympus!" and when St. Paul, preaching on Mars Hill, used the words " as certain of your own poets have said, ' for we are His offspring,' " * the men to whom he spoke recognized, as we should do if one were to quote a line from Wordsworth, that line in Aratus which he in turn had borrowed from his greater predecessor Cleanthes. Has it ever occurred to you, now, to think of the spell which such hymns must have exercised, or those others of Anacreon, of Catullus, and of Horace which Roman soldiers, or scholars, or plebeians who had turned to Christ had heard long before in some imperial temple or sanctuary? These were the things that touched the heart, and stirred the blood, and moved the deepest emotions. And so, with a very real wisdom, the Church in her first days called into her service the Christian Hymn, and in his letters to the Churches in Ephesus and in

---

* Acts xvii. 28.

Colosse, where St. Paul enjoins those to whom he writes to speak or to admonish (remind, rather) one another " in psalms and hymns and spiritual songs," we find the beginnings of that universal custom which was soon to spread throughout the Christian world. " The disciples," the author of the Book of the Acts of the Apostles tells us, " were called Christians first at Antioch;"* and a very ancient and beautiful tradition, preserved by the historian Socrates, maintains that Ignatius, who suffered martyrdom A. D. 107, and who must therefore have been very close to, if not contemporary with the Apostle St. John, was led by a vision or dream of Angels, singing hymns antiphonally to the Holy Trinity, to introduce the antiphonal singing of hymns into the Church at Antioch, from which it spread quickly to other churches. How widely the custom spread and how deeply it became rooted is indicated in a somewhat curious way by the fact that the council of the Syrian Church, which two centuries later deposed Paul of Samosata from that same see of Antioch, did so, among other reasons, because he had prohibited the use of hymns to Christ written by

---

* Acts xi. 26.

uninspired writers. Indeed, the time was not long in coming when, in the Eastern Church, the singing of hymns came to have a very distinct polemic significance, and there is no more dramatic page in the somewhat turbulent history of the Arian Controversy than that which tells how the disciples of Arius, when St. John Chrysostom was raised to the Metropolitan See of Constantinople, were wont, having no places of worship within the walls of the city, to come into it on Saturdays, Sundays, and the greater festivals, and, assembling in places of public resort, sing songs ridiculing the orthodox faith and extolling their own. It was because Chrysostom apprehended that this heterodox hymn-singing might mislead and pervert the simple-minded among his flock, that, with the help of Eudoxia, Empress of Arcadius, he organized a system of nightly processional hymn-singing, with silver crosses, wax candles, and other features of ceremonial pomp; out of which grew the singing of hymns in connection with certain solemnities at night, which became before long an established institution. How vast it grew to be is indicated by the fact that the late Dr. John Mason Neale computed the number of hymns in the earlier service books of the Greek Church to be nearly five thousand, a fact which may be consoling to those who object, in our own hymnal, to so many as five hundred!

The same reasons which had been influential in making the use of hymns to be so early so conspicuous a feature in the Eastern Church were at work in the West; and in the Western or Latin Church the movement was hastened by an incident of exceptional and even pathetic character. Undoubtedly the two great leaders in this matter were St. Hilary of Poitiers, and St. Ambrose. Of the latter you are to hear from another, but of St. Hilary it may be mentioned that he was banished from his see A. D. 356, and was absent from it in Asia Minor for about four years. During those four years St. Jerome, who was near middle life when St. Hilary died, and who had lived in and near his diocese, tells us that he wrote a book of hymns. His residence in the East, where he had taken part in one of the Councils of the Eastern Church, had doubtless familiarized him with its worship, in which the singing of hymns bore so large a part; and it was quite natural that he should turn, in his enforced leisure, to so kindred an occupation as their composition. Already, in his western home, as Jerome elsewhere mentions, the use of sacred song had become the habit of the people, and one who " went into the fields might hear the ploughman at his hallelujahs, the mower at his hymns, and the vine-dressers singing David's psalms."

It was a custom of profound and far-reaching influence which thus grew up in the Church of the West; and the evolution of the hymn in the form substantially in which we have it to-day is one of the most interesting studies in the development of Western Christianity. The foremost authority, I venture to think, upon this subject—one to whom another whom I have already mentioned, Dr. John Mason Neale, refers as "the first Victorian scholar in England and probably in Europe," the late Archbishop of Dublin, Dr. Trench—has pointed out, with a rare and penetrating acumen,* that " there is one very obvious and yet very noteworthy difference between the Christian literature of the Greek and Roman world, on the one side, and all other and later Christian literatures on the other, namely, that the Greek and Latin literatures of Christian authorship were, so to speak, a new budding and blossoming out of an old

---

* Sacred Latin Poetry, p. 3 *et seq.*

stock which, when the Church was founded, had already put forth, or was in the act of putting forth, all which, in the natural order of things, and but for the quickening breath of a new and unexpected life, it could ever have unfolded. They are as a second and later spring coming in the rear of the timelier and the first. For that task which the new religion had to accomplish in all other regions of man's life it had also to accomplish in this. It was not granted to it at first entirely to make or mould a society of its own. A harder task was assigned to it—being, as it was, superinduced on a society which had long before come into existence, and had gradually assumed the conditions which it now wore under very different conditions and in obedience to very different influences. Of this it had to make the best that it could; not only to reject and put under ban that in it which was absolutely incurable, and which directly contradicted its fundamental idea, but, of the rest, to assimilate to itself what was capable of assimilation, to transmute what was willing to be transmuted; to consecrate what was prepared to receive from it a higher consecration, and altogether to adjust, not always with perfect success, but as best it might, often at the cost of much forbearance and self-sacrifice, its relations to the old which had grown up under heathen auspices" and in a heathen atmosphere.

This, I say, was what the new religion had to do with reference to the family, the state, social intercourse, art, commerce, in one word, all that makes up man's moral and intellectual life. It had the same thing to do with heathen literature —its forms, its traditions, its modes of expression. The task was quite a different one, as Trench has shown, in the case of other and more modern peoples. These, indeed, had a language, and in some meagre sense a literature. But both were relatively young and plastic, and it is not too much to say that Christianity moulded and dominated them rather than they affected or influenced it.

But it was otherwise with the Latin tongue. That, "when the Church arose, requiring of it to be the organ of the Divine Word, to tell out all the new and as yet undreamt of life that was stirring in her breast; demanding of it that it should reach her needs—needs that had hardly or not at all existed while the language was in process of formation — that was already full-formed and had reached its climacteric." The Church could not therefore create a Latin tongue to be the vehicle of communication with those various peoples, under the rule of the vast Empire of Rome, to whom she came. She had to take the Latin tongue as she found it, and use it and readjust it, and enrich and, above all, popularize it, to be the devotional language of the civilized world. Nothing, I repeat, is more profoundly interesting or more profoundly impressive than the way in which she did so. No language of superlative can exaggerate the splendor and beauty of classic poetry, whether Grecian or Roman. The high authority whom I have already quoted, concluding his exquisite essay on sacred Latin poetry, says of it in substance that, beautiful as some of it is, it must still leave " the great masterpieces of Greece and Rome forever without a peer." That is undoubtedly true. There has been but one Homer, but one Virgil, but one Pindar, but one Horace. But, exquisite as were the forms in which Latin verse had cast itself, it did not take a great while for the Church to discover that it was ill-suited to the higher uses for which she sought rhythmical and poetical forms of expression. If there were no other and subtler reason, there remained the evil of its associations. Who could sing a Christian hymn in a metre which Catullus had made familiar?

Who could worship Christ with rhythms that had been prostituted to the vilest heathen rites? And there was yet another reason for some sort of change, which had in it a most inspiring significance. If a Latin hexameter verse is not within the reach of anyone to whom I speak this afternoon, let such an one get hold of Arthur Hugh Clough's charming poem, "The Bothie of Tober-na-Vuolich," which is written in English hexameters. There is undoubtedly an element of attraction in that famous classic metre. But no one would for a moment think of casting into such a form a hymn or poem meant for the use of the great mass of the people. It is pre-eminently a scholar's metre, with a charm too subtle and elusive to appeal to any other than a scholar's ear. And so of all the rest. When to-day one reads a sacred hymn or poem in sapphics, or alcaics, or hendecasyllables, there is in it the double incongruity of the aroma of its heathen associations, and the obscurity of its scholastic niceties.

I have dealt upon this point at what you may regard as disproportionate length, because it is the porch through which a very large and mightily influential element of Christian worship passed out of the dominion of classic forms of verse into those others with which to-day we are most of all familiar. What, now, is it in these which most of all helps to fix them in the memory and to make the people sing them? It is, I maintain, that distinctive and (in contrast with classic forms) comparatively modern feature which distinguishes them as rhythmical rather than merely metrical, and which culminated ultimately in the terminal assonance or consonance which we know as rhyme. I do not pretend to claim, as some writers have done, either that this is an exclusively distinctive feature of sacred Latin verse, or that its existence elsewhere in modern literature is owing wholly to the influence of sacred Latin poetry. A very superficial examination of the evidence in the case must convince one that rhymed verse is as old as Persian poetry, and that instances of it may be found in Chinese and Sanscrit and in Arabic poems, as well as in the *Andromache* of Ennius, and other Latin poets; and as Plutarch has shown, even in Homer itself—sources which all of them have influenced later scholars as well as the splendid treasure-house of Latin hymnology. But what I do maintain is that it was in this connection that rhymed verse took on its largest distinction, and rose at length to singular heights of grace and beauty. And I do not think that one need search far to explain it. Mr. Guest, in his " History of English Rhythms," * has said that rhyme " is not, as is sometimes asserted, a mere ornament; it marks and defines the accent, and thereby strengthens and supports the rhythm. Its advantages have been felt so strongly that no people has ever adopted an accentual rhythm without also adopting rhyme." And for this I believe that there is a very profound reason. Have you ever lain awake at night by the sea, and listened to the successive breaking of the waves upon the shore, or, in travel, have you ever noted the effect upon the mind of the *ictus* of the rails, as the wheels of your car, one after another, struck them and left them? In both these cases there was rhythm, the one that of nature, the other that of mechanical art; but both producing the same effect, of which I think the finest instance in our own tongue is that matchless poem of Tennyson's,

> " Break, Break, Break,
> On thy cold gray stones, O sea,
> And I would that my tongue could utter
> The thoughts that arise in me ! "

---

* Vol. i., p. 116.

Can anyone doubt that here the rhythmic regulated recurrence—the iterance of substantially the same sound at substantially the same interval—made the poem, and made it because in the human intelligence there is something responsive to rhythmic and periodic sounds speaking " of order, proportion, purpose "—and so, of the great Soul that throbs behind all this marshalled pageantry of nature, and who is himself the God of a divine order, proportion, purpose? Ewald, in his " Poetic Books of the Old Testament," * has a passage which puts this thought with singular and characteristic force. " A stream of words and images, an impetuous diction, a movement which, in the first violence, seems to know no bounds nor control—such is the earliest manifestation of poetic diction. But a diction which should only continue in this its earliest movement, and hurry onward without bounds and without measure, would soon destroy its own beauty, even its very life. Yea, rather the more living and overflowing this onward movement is, by so much the more needful the restraint and the limitation, the counteraction and tranquillization of this becomes. This

---

* Vol. i., p. 57.

mighty inspiration and expiration; this rise, with its commensurate fall; this advance in symmetrical diction, which shall combine rest and motion with one another, and mutually reconcile them; this is rhythm or regulated beautiful movement." Could there be more apt or suggestive intimation of the way in which, in the history of Western Christianity, hymnody gathered up the young and fervid devotional life of earlier ages, and, as the centuries advanced, gave it unceasingly full, and fervid, and felicitous expression?

It is of one particular illustration of it that I am more especially to speak this afternoon. It cannot be claimed that it is the greatest or most beautiful of Latin hymns, nor yet the most venerable in age, or distinguished as to authorship. The metrical hymns of St. Hilary or St. Ambrose long preceded it, as did the beautiful hymns of Prudentius, who, it may interest my brethren of the laity to know, was himself a Spanish layman, born in Saragossa in A.D. 348, and a contemporary of Hilary and Ambrose.

The Hymn which, in two forms, we find in our Office for the Ordination of Priests and that for "Ordaining and Consecrating" Bishops is of a much later date. It has been ascribed to St.

Ambrose, but it is not claimed by his Benedictine editors, and there is probably no better warrant for the claim than that to Ambrose a great multitude of Latin hymns were ascribed in times subsequent to his own, simply because they had evidently been composed after the model and pattern of hymns of which undoubtedly he was the author.* A far more common and popular belief is that which has attributed the hymn to the Emperor Charlemagne. There is little doubt that this remarkable historical personage, who exercised so extraordinary an influence in the somewhat forceful conversion of the Gothic nations, was a writer of hymns, and that his character was distinguished by a marked devotional element; but there is even less doubt that, in this case, his identity has been confounded with that of another sovereign, his grandson Charles the Bald. In our Office for the Burial of the Dead there is an anthem, " Man that is born of a Woman," which is undoubtedly the composition of a monk of St. Gall in Switzerland, Notker by name, to whom also, I may mention in passing, some of the best authorities trace the great hymn " Dies Iræ." Of this saint and scholar there

---

* See note A., p. 160.

survives a biography written in the thirteenth century by Ekkehard. This work, as the late Lord Selborne (better known to most of us as Sir Roundell Palmer), to whom in this connection I am glad to own my large indebtedness, has pointed out, was written in the same Benedictine monastery to which Notker had belonged, and the " biographer relates that Notker —a man of gentle, contemplative nature, observant of all around him, and accustomed to find spiritual and poetical suggestions in common sights and sounds — was moved by the sound of a mill-wheel (an illustration, by the way, of what I have already referred to) to compose his " sequence" on the Holy Spirit, " Sancti Spiritus adsit nobis gratia " ("Present with us ever be the Holy Spirit's grace "), and that, when finished, he sent it as a present to the " Emperor Charles," who, in return, sent him back by the same messenger the hymn " Veni Creator " which (says Ekkehard) the same Spirit had inspired him to write (" Sibi idem Spiritus insperaverat "). " If this story," says Lord Selborne, " is to be credited—and from its circumstantial and almost dramatic character it has an air of truth—the author of ' Veni Creator ' was not Charlemagne, but his grandson, Charles the

THE HYMNS OF THE ORDINAL. 149

Bold, who succeeded to the royal crown in A. D. 840 (about the time when Notker was born) and to the imperial in 875. Notker himself long survived that emperor and died in 912." * An additional though indirect confirmation of this authorship is the fact that this hymn has, for nearly a thousand years, been used not only in public worship, but in connection with the coronation of kings, the celebration of synods, and other kindred solemnities. We have already sung the shorter of the two versions of the "Veni Creator," and both are in your Prayer-books in the Office for the Ordination of Priests, so that I need not repeat them here. The second or longer translation is the older, and is supposed to have been made by Archbishop Cranmer in connection with the revision of the Ordinal by the Commission, of which he was a member and probably the guiding spirit. The shorter version, which stands first in the Office, and which is most commonly used, was not introduced until 1662, and Blunt is authority for saying that it was made by the poet Dryden. The earlier or longer translation by Cranmer is perhaps open to the charge of being, in some respects, a para-

---

* Lord Selborne, Hymns. Encyc. Brit., vol. xii., p. 583.

phrase rather than a translation, though it must be owned that the first two lines of each of the sixteen verses of which it is composed adhere closely to the Latin original. Dryden's translation gains undoubtedly in compactness, but there is in some of the verses of the longer translation, a singular quaintness and almost rustic beauty which have a very real charm of their own.

Neither of them, however, at all brings over into our less fluid and eloquent tongue the native grace and exquisite rhythm of the Latin original. That, indeed, we may not hope to secure, in the matter of verse, by any translation by any whatsoever most gifted hand. A language is like a landscape; you can reproduce it upon canvas, but you cannot transplant it. And the figure the better serves my purpose because there is in speech, as in scenery, a light and aroma of its own. These are too subtle for chemical analysis or transmutation. All the airs of Greece pulse through the strains of Homer; but a French translation of Shakespeare is like an Italian version of Pilgrim's Progress, an echo, not the strain itself. I shall therefore venture to read this great Latin hymn in the original, even at the cost of being charged with a cheap pedantry for doing so, just because in no other way can you so easily detect in it what I have endeavored to make plain to you as to the grace and charm of the form of Sacred Latin verse; remembering, moreover, that everyone of you has, at this moment, the two English versions of it within easy reach of your hand. The version which I quote is from Trench's matchless work on "Sacred Latin Poetry," * and is fuller, and, I apprehend, more accurate, than any other:

> Veni Creator Spiritus,
> Mentes tuorum visita,
> Imple supernâ gratiâ
> Quæ to creasti pectora.
>
> Qui Paraclitus diceris,
> Altissimi donum Dei,
> Fons vivus, ignis, caritas,
> Et spiritalis unctio.
>
> Tu septiformis munere
> Dextræ Dei tu digitus,
> Tu rite promissum Patris,
> Sermone ditans guttura.
>
> Accende lumen sensibus,
> Infund(e) amorem cordibus,
> Irfirma nostri corporis
> Virtute firmans perpeti.

---

* Pp. 167-169.

Hostem repellas longius,
Pacemque dones protinus,
Ductore sic te prævio
Vitémus omne noxium.

Da gaudiorum præmia,
Da gratiarum munera,
Dissolve litis vincula,
Adstringe pacis fœdera.

Per te sciamus da, Patrem,
Noscamus atque Filium,
Te utriusque Spiritum
Credamus omni tempore.

Sit laus Patri cum Filio,
Sancto simul Paraclito,
Nobisque mittat Filius
Charisma Sancti Spiritûs.*

An illustration or two will show how closely this hymn follows the teachings of Holy Scripture and with what singular felicity a wide reference to its various utterances as to the office and work of the Holy Ghost is packed into the narrow compass of a few lines. In the second verse there occur the two lines,

"*Fons vivus, ignis, caritas,
Et spiritalis unctio,*"

---

* See Note B, page 160.

which the second or fuller and (in this instance) closer translation renders:

> "The fountain and the living spring
> Of joy celestial,
> The fire so bright, the love so sweet,
> The unction spiritual."

But this is not mere rhetoric. We turn from the "fons vivus," "the fountain and the living spring," to St. John's Gospel and we read:* " In the last day, that great day of the feast Jesus stood and cried saying, 'If any man thirst let him come unto me, and drink. He that believeth on me, as the Scripture saith, out of him shall flow rivers of living water." Or we ask for what "ignis," "the fire so bright," stands, and we turn to St. Luke's Gospel and read: " I am come to send fire on the earth; and what will I, if it be already kindled?" † The Latin caritas (" the love so sweet," as it is rendered) carries us straightway to those words of St. Paul's in his letter to the Church at Rome: " The love of God is shed abroad in our hearts by the Holy Ghost which is given us;" ‡ and the Latin " unctio," to those

---

* St. John vii. 37, 38.
† St. Luke xii. 49.
‡ Romans v. 5.

words in St. John's First Epistle General, "Ye have an unction from the Holy One," and "the anointing which ye have received abideth in you and ye need not that any man should teach you," for "the same anointing teacheth you all things." *

I may not, within these narrow limits, pursue further this exegetical line of comment; but before I dismiss it I may venture perhaps to call your attention to one singularly exquisite and suggestive line in this noble hymn which reveals at once the spiritual perception of its author, and an evident and intimate knowledge of the Bible in an age which is least credited with it; and that, on the part of one from whom in these days, I fear, it would be least expected. It is found in the third stanza and is second in the couplet,

"Tu septiformis munere,
Dextræ Dei tu digitus,"

which the fuller English version renders,

"Thou in thy gifts art manifold,
By them Christ's Church doth stand,
In faithful hearts thou writest thy law,
The finger of God's hand."

---

* 1 John ii. 20, 27.

That is, the Holy Ghost is the finger, as it were, of God's hand, by which finger He writes His law in the hearts of men. Now, there can be no doubt as to where the writer of this hymn derived this image. In St. Luke's Gospel * there is a scene between Christ and His critics in which He uses the words " If I with the finger of God cast out devils, no doubt the kingdom of God is come upon you." But that which interprets the phrase " the finger of God " is plainly the parallel passage in St. Matthew's Gospel † where the phrase is " If I cast out devils by the Spirit of God, then the kingdom of God is come unto you." The finger thus becomes the image of the work of the Holy Ghost in transferring, fixing, and engraving, so to speak, spiritual impressions. " Thou writest." St. Augustine, in his Commentary on the ninetieth Psalm, carries the thought a step farther with penetrating and yet not too subtle suggestiveness. " By the Holy Spirit of God," he says substantially, " the gifts of God are distributed, and accomplish thus their diverse work; and yet as the fingers of the hand are parts of one whole, and are joined to-

---

* St. Luke xi. 20.
† St. Matthew xii. 28.

gether in one hand, even so the various gifts and operations of the Spirit return for their source to one centre, and are united in one root," * And in the *De Civitatis Dei* † there is a fine passage in which Augustine points out how the phrase which Christ uses in speaking of the work of the Holy Ghost recalls the tables of the elder law written with the finger of God. Certainly such imagery invests the act of the laying on of hands with a new august solemnity. The human instrument becomes a veritable symbol of the divine, and no poor superstition as to the power of a merely magical touch can cloud or belittle its great and most solemn import.

I would that these limits allowed me to pursue further this line of comment. But though I may not do so, I cannot leave it without calling your attention to a certain largeness in the tone of this ancient hymn which is not its least noble characteristic. In the second couplet of the sixth verse occur the lines:

> " Dissolve litis vincula,
> Adstringe pacis fœdera." ‡

---

* St. Augustine, Enarr. 2d, Ps. xc., Ps. cxliii.
† *De Civitatis Dei*, 1, 16, c. 43.
‡ See Note C, page 160.

which the earlier translation has not unworthily rendered,

> " Of strife and of dissension
> Dissolve, O Lord, the bands,
> And knit the knots of peace and love
> Throughout all Christian lands."

Surely that is a conception worthy not only of a great sovereign, but of a great soul! We go back in imagination to the age and to the ruler with which it was connected. How elementary and almost barbaric it was in much, if not most, that most people esteem to-day, as making up what they call civilization. How bare life was of much that enriches our life—how meagre its literature, how scanty its means of communication, how grotesque many of its superstitions, how cruel much of its intolerance, how simple, if not childish, its faith. For nearly four centuries the work of a mediæval monk, the Franciscan, Bartholomew, on "The Properties of Thing,"* which taught "If a crocodile findeth a man by the water's brim, he slayeth him, and then he weepeth over him, and swalloweth him," was the standard work of natural history.

---

* See White's History of the Warfare of Science with Theology, pp. 33–36.

For a much longer period the great mass of people lived and died in a condition of intellectual ignorance which to-day would disgrace the youngest schoolboy. And yet, out of the midst of such ignorance there arose a type of Christian character, a love of devout learning, a passion, often, for personal sanctity of which I fear the times in which we live are not over-full. A Christian saint and scholar occupies his leisure hours in writing a Christian hymn in the Latin tongue, and then sends it to his sovereign. His sovereign, busy with the cares of state, with wars and campaigns, and all the grave concerns of a great empire, finds time not only to acknowledge the courtesy, but to return it, and to return it in such kind that the Church takes up the hymn which this king wrote a thousand years ago, and hands it on and down through all the changing centuries to tell up into the hearkening ear of God that never-ending need alike of priests and people which is, of all other needs, the greatest! One turns from such an age and such rulers to our own. We have gained much since then, we say. There is more light, more knowledge, more various learning, less superstition, less priestcraft, less idolatry, less cruelty, less tyranny, less suffering in the world now. I hope so. But how about the vision of the eternal? A man may be very clever about the Mosaic cosmogony, about astronomy, about the liberties of the people—his vision may have been so widened that he can take in a far wider area of facts from which to generalize than the earlier centuries ever dreamed of. How is it when one comes to look up? "I have turned toward the heavens," said the French astronomer La Lande, "the most powerful telescope that ever was constructed, and there is nothing beyond them!" But Stephen could say, even while the stones crushed the life out of his mangled body, "I see heaven opened and the Son of Man standing on the right hand of God!" What gave to him that strange and transcendent power of upward vision? Ah! it was that for which the Church cries aloud when her sons kneel at her altar and ask for her Apostolic commission:

> "O Holy Ghost into our minds
> Send down thy heavenly light.
> Kindle our hearts with fervent zeal
> To serve God day and night!"

It is this, and this alone, which makes a ministry of power. May she never cease to pray for it, and may she never be without it!

Note A. Mention ought not to be wholly omitted of the tradition which ascribes this hymn to Gregory the Great, on the following grounds:
1. Its correspondence with his writings generally, and especially with hymns known to be his.
2. Its classical metre with occasional rhymes.
3. The correct quantity of the penultimate of *Paraclites*, as showing a knowledge of Greek.

These arguments have undoubtedly a certain force; but it is highly improbable that a writer of such eminence could have written a hymn in the sixth century which, for four or five hundred years no one dreamed of attributing to him. Bede, in his *De Arte metrica*, makes no mention of it, and apart from subjective grounds there is no warrant for ascribing the hymn to Gregory. (See Dict. Hymnol., Julian, p. 1208.)

Note B. It cannot be denied that the doxology in this hymn is probably of later date than the hymn itself. This is indicated by the variations, in this particular, of different versions of the Hymn. The *Durham Hymnal* gives:

> Sit laus Patri cum Genito,
> Amborum et Paraclito,
> Proles ut hunc promiserat,
> Nobis modoque tribuat.

In the Roman Breviary of 1570 and 1632, the doxology reads:

> Deo Patri sit gloria
> Et Filio, Qui a mortuis
> Surrexit ac Paraclito,
> In sempiterna (sacculorum) sæcula.

Note C. An authority already quoted (see Note A) the Reverend John Julian, maintains that the stanza of which these lines form a part is an addition to the original text, and gives a list of early authorities in which it is wanting. On the other hand, it is to be found in two manuscripts in the Bodleian Library, one of the twelfth and the other of the thirteenth century, and in some of the earliest printed books, such as the Basel Breviary. In any case, it is an instance in which one may be glad that our Anglican Mother in retaining it, has given us the benefit of the doubt. Whether certainly original or not, it is distinctly an "enrichment."

II

Te Deum Laudamus.

LECTURE V.

THE REV. WILLIAM R. HUNTINGTON, D.D.
Rector of Grace Church.

TE DEUM LAUDAMUS.

We have met together to study the most wonderful of all the sacred songs of Christendom—the Te Deum.

The wonder of it is the wonder of variety. No rival composition can compare with the Te Deum in point of range and sweep. None is tangent to the deeper thought of man at so many points. Other hymns may surpass it in the exhibition of this or that phase of feeling, but there is none that combines as this combines all the elements that enter into a Christian's concept of religion. The Te Deum is an orchestra in which no single instrument is lacking; first or last, every chord is struck, every note sounded. The soul listens and is satisfied; not one of her large demands has been dishonored. The splendid exultancy of the Magnificat, the tender plaintiveness of Nunc dimittis, the cosmic harmonies of the Benedicite, the clear, bell-like tone of the song of Zacharias, all seem to find congress and unison in what has been well called *Hymnus Optimus*, the best of hymns.

This characteristic of the Te Deum upon which I have fastened first, its comprehensiveness, is closely connected with what scholars now conceive to have been the origin of the composition. Like many another ancient document, the Te Deum, subjected to the search-light of criticism, has been found to be a product of growth. It may go against the grain with many of us to surrender the pleasing old tradition which would have it that the hymn was extemporized by St. Ambrose and St. Augustine at the font; the two singing it antiphonally as they stood; but since the story can be traced no farther than the ninth century, while the hymn itself goes back certainly to the fifth, possibly even to the fourth, we shall have to subordinate sentiment to probability, and accept the findings of scholarship without murmur.

The best authorities upon the points of authorship and date, are, among Germans, Daniel, the learned compiler of the *Thesaurus Hymnologicus;* and, among Englishmen, Dr. Swainson, late

Margaret Professor of Divinity in the University of Cambridge, the present accomplished Bishop of Salisbury, and Prebendary Gibson of the Cathedral Chapter of Wells. Almost all of what I have to say in this lecture upon the purely historical and antiquarian features of the subject in hand I say upon the warrant of one or other of these eminent liturgical scholars. For the analysis and the interpretation alone do I make any claim to originality of treatment, though even, as respects analysis and interpretation, originality will, I am quite aware, be deprecated by those who hold fondly to the maxim that whatever is new in theology is false.

The Te Deum as a whole is emphatically a hymn of the Western Church. The East, in so far as it knows it at all, knows it only in its Latin form. And yet, curiously enough, the first ten out of the twenty-nine verses which constitute the hymn as we have it, are found standing by themselves under a Greek guise in no fewer than four important manuscripts. This does not prove that the ten verses in question had a Greek origin, for they may have been translated from the Latin into the Greek, but it does make highly probable the supposition that this opening portion was once a distinct hymn, used independently of what now follows it. In fact, to this conclusion a critical study of the structure of the hymn might of itself lead us, quite independently of the linguistic argument, for it is evident to any one intelligently following the Te Deum in public worship, that when we reach the ejaculation " Thou art the King of Glory, O Christ," we enter, as it were, upon a new stage, make a fresh start, begin again.

Down to this point, the hymn has been one of simple adoration addressed to God as such— " We praise Thee, O God; we acknowledge Thee to be the Lord." How this sentiment is expanded so as to make it cover both the Old Testament and the New Testament conceptions of the nature of Deity we shall consider presently, for the moment I am simply calling attention to one of the two great lines of cleavage which determine the structure of the composition as a whole.

The hymn to Christ which follows the confession of the Trinity ends with the twenty-first verse, culminating in the words Make them to be numbered or rewarded (according as we read " numerari " or " munerari " in the Latin), with thy Saints in Glory everlasting.

The remaining eight verses of the canticle are, with two exceptions, all of them supplicatory in their character, and are simply an echo of the Psalter. These, like the opening verses, are addressed to Almighty God in His character of Ruler and Father of His people.

This simple analysis will suffice to prepare us for an interpretative study of the text. You see the whole tract of the Te Deum lying spread out before you in its threefold unity, with first, as we may say, an act of worship, next an act of faith, and last an act of supplication. Let us now go on to study these several acts or movements in their order, noting what is most admirable or curious in each, and by scrutinizing the purport of the sentences in severalty prepare ourselves the better to appreciate the finished whole.

I. The dominant note of the entire first section is sounded in the opening words, "We praise," *laudamus*.

We praise thee, O God: we acknowledge thee to be the Lord.
All the earth doth worship thee: the Father everlasting.
To thee all Angels cry aloud: the Heavens and all the Powers therein;
To thee Cherubim and Seraphim: continually do cry,
Holy, Holy, Holy: Lord God of Sabaoth.
Heaven and earth are full: of the Majesty of thy glory.

Here we have adoration pure and simple; praise for its own sake. To know how to render this is a rare accomplishment. Souls capable of attaining to it are capable of the best, since honest praise is the outcome of an absolute unselfishness. And yet, when we think of it, adoration ought not to be such a difficult spiritual exercise. If only we were single-hearted, nothing would seem to us more natural than praise. We are so made that whenever we discern excellency, whether in persons or things, our impulse is to speak out the joy stirred in us by the sight. This impulse never fails to assert itself except when counteracted either by an inveterate sluggishness of temper or else by the active forces of jealousy and hatred. And yet, even when it has been thwarted, or suppressed, there is the instinct still within us prompting us to express joy whenever anything beautiful or glorious crosses the field of vision, whether in that atmosphere which covers the earth as with a garment or in that more subtile ether where only spiritual eyesight tells. Praise is the form of expression which this joy-instinct seeks whenever what has roused the feeling has in it the personal element. Things we can admire; but only actions, or the persons from whom actions spring, can we praise. We admire the statue, we praise the sculptor.

In worship we exercise toward God the same feelings and affections that bind us to our fellowmen. Unless we allowed ourselves to do this, religion would be struck dumb. Of course, it may be urged that God stands in no need of our adoration, that since He is in heaven and we upon earth, any ascription of praise to Him on our part is superfluous, or worse than superfluous. This remonstrance has the more color to it because we know that even in our relations to one another a great disparity of social or intellectual rank sometimes silences the voice of praise. "What cares he," we say to ourselves, of some one greatly our superior, "What cares he for my praise or for my blame? He is so far up above my level that for me to attempt or to presume to praise him would be simply an impertinence."

Reasoning of this sort, when applied to worship, chills the very blood in religion's veins; but happily the fallacy of it is not far to seek. The thing which hinders the man of high degree from welcoming and appreciating the praise of the man of low degree is pride. Blot pride altogether out of your mind's image of the Divine Majesty, and there ceases to be any difficulty in supposing praise, even the poor praise of mortal men, to be acceptable with God. In fact, when we come to think of it, our praise is the only thing we have that we can give Him. Everything else is His already.

Of course it is easy to sneer at this mode of conceiving our duty toward God as anthropomorphic. But is it not a sheer necessity that all our discourse of the Almighty should utter itself in anthropomorphic, or, to use plainer English, in humanized speech? We have no other; so long as we depend for our vocabulary upon the sights and sounds of this world present we need expect no other. The body of language with which all human thought is clothed upon is a body terrestrial, and if we are to utter ourselves to God at all we must do so in forms of words not wholly unlike those we should employ were we addressing the purest, wisest, worthiest of men. If we praise a liberator of nations for his prowess, if we praise a painter for his picture, if we praise a poet for his song, so must we be willing, unless we propose to dispense with articulate speech altogether in our religious life, to praise God for His mighty acts, to praise Him according to His excellent greatness.

No, so far as we who profess and call ourselves Christians are concerned, it is not any quibble about God's unwillingness to receive praise that troubles us, it is rather our own mortifying incapacity to render praise. But this is just where the Te Deum comes in to help us with its splendid confidence in creation's capacity to adore. What a proud universal it is, that second verse, "All the earth doth worship thee." We detect no falsetto in that note. Clearly the first singer of this song was a believer who believed with all his heart, with all his mind, with all his soul, and with all his strength. Even in the best religious poetry of our own day, from Matthew Arnold's to Cardinal Newman's, there lurks a gentle tone of incertitude; but no such blemish mars this virile note. For the moment, unbelief, half-belief, misbelief, seem, all of them, forgotten, and we picture the great round world to ourselves as a converted, a God-fearing, God-serving, God-loving world; every denizen of it ready and eager to give thanks—All the earth doth worship Thee.

And then, too, how encouraging, how uplifting is this proud alliance with the invisible choirs, this joining forces with all angels, all heavens, and all powers, with cherubim and seraphim, yes, with whatever creature or child of God has right anywhere in God's wide universe to lift that full Ter Sanctus in which man's adoration everywhere must culminate, Holy, Holy, Holy, Lord God of Hosts. Great is the wealth of comfort hidden in the thought that it is possible thus to become confederate with those who know how to worship even if we do not. It is a relief, moreover, to be reminded that we are not the only ones in all God's worlds upon whom the responsibility of giving praise rests. Your voice or mine may falter, your thoughts or mine may wander, but there is really no lull perceptible in the full-voiced anthem. The heavenly choruses sing on. All are not wavering though we waver, all are not failing though we fail; but somewhere in the great temple of the divine presence they who excel in strength are making our weakness good.

Close upon this representation of the worshipping universe follows the companion picture of the worshipping Church of Christ. Thus far every thing has been proceeding upon the level of a theological territory which Jew and Christian hold in common. We seldom stop to think, and it is well that we should, now and then, be reminded how broad that territory is. The Church and the Synagogue are co-inheritors of a treasure larger than is commonly supposed. We sing Thomas Olivers' majestic hymn,

> The God of Abraham praise,
> Who reigns enthroned above,

with no sense of incongruity; and yet it is (so Julian the hymnologist assures us), only a " free rendering " of an old doxology which " rehearses in metrical form the thirteen articles of the Hebrew Creed." Yes, their God is our God. " For the hope of Israel," cries Paul, " I am bound with this chain." And it was " in the year that King Uzziah died," seven hundred years before Christ, that Isaiah heard the " Holy, Holy, Holy," sung.

Christianity is not the negation of Judaism, it is rather Judaism plus the new truths brought into the world through the incarnation of the Son of God. So here in the opening sentences of the Te Deum, after we have laid the foundation of praise in words to which Noah, Daniel, and Job might have assented, after we have recognized as fellow-worshippers those whose names and titles were as dear to the true believers of the elder world as they are to us of Christian times, we go on to recognize and to adopt what is special to the New Testament, and to affirm of the Apostles, Prophets, and Martyrs of the Lord Jesus, that they as well as the Angels and the Powers, the Cherubs and Seraphs, have lot and part in this great task of praise. Notice the processional character of the whole picture. First, the glorious company of the Apostles moving with that dignified tread which befits leaders; next the Prophets, Christian prophets as I interpret the meaning here, such prophets as we read of in the Book of Acts and in the Epistles to the Corinthians, the prophets of the New Dispensation, and, following these, the white-robed Martyrs, the men who at the cost of their own lives have been brave to witness a good confession, and have sealed their testimony with their blood. These three seem by themselves a little army, and yet they are but serving as escort and guard of honor to a vast host that stretches out, rank after rank, over the fields of time as far as eye can see, its name the generous one of " Holy Church throughout all the world."

Flandrin, one of the very few of the religiously minded among the great French artists of our time, has caught the spirit of this portion of the Te Deum in his decorative treatment of the frieze in one of the churches of Paris. Beginning with St. Peter and St. Paul, he leads the long column of the faithful completely around the building. Kings marching on foot, confessors with the emblems of their suffering, bishops and doctors of the faith, mothers carrying their babies on their breasts and leading little children by the hand, all are there making up the fulness of the blessed company of the faithful in Christ Jesus.

Pause a moment here to consider why it is that apostles, prophets, and martyrs should be singled out for an especially honorable position at the front. Why do we see them marching at the head of the column, like a field officer's staff a few feet in advance of the rank and file? For this reason, I am disposed to think, namely, that in their characters, as these are defined by their titles, prophets, apostles, and martyrs completely represent the whole human side of religion. The three great elements of the godly life, as man takes cognizance of godliness, are vision, action, and passion. Vision comes first. In order so much as to begin to be religious we must catch at least some glimpse of the Divine Majesty, we must have an inkling, if no more, of what God is like. Here is where the function of the prophet comes in. The prophet is one who has been privileged to discern the truth of God, and who, because he has discerned it, is able to communicate it to others. The Seer sees, and having seen speaks and tells. It is plain, therefore, that without prophecy, or the unveiling of the truth of God, religion, or the service of God, cannot so much as begin. But no sooner has the heavenly vision been vouchsafed than action, the second of the three great elements of religion, is seen to be in order. Thus we have, along with our prophets or men of vision, apostles or men of action, and not only are the apostles associated with the prophets, they are also in large measure dependent on them for guidance. " Go into the city," says the voice of Christ to the astonished Saul, " Go into the city and it shall be told thee what thou shalt do." The destined apostle, that is to say, must have the help of the prophet before he can see his path. But not action only, there is the third element, passion, or suffering, and this the martyrs represent. Saul, singled out, in the providence of God, to become martyr and apostle in one, went into the city as he was bid, and it was showed him there not only what he must do but also what great things he should suffer for Christ's sake. Yes, we need them all in the Church of God, all three of the contingents, the goodly one, the glorious one, and the white-robed one; we need them and we have them. Did you ever notice that this whole portion of the Te Deum is in the present tense? It does not read "have praised thee;" it does not read "shall praise thee," it reads simply "praise thee." This co-operant adoration is a thing that is forever going on; there is no pause or lull; apostles, prophets, martyrs are still bringing day by day their tribute. We hear a great deal, and rightly enough, of Apostolical Succession; but what of the succession of the prophets and the succession of the martyrs? Are not they real also? Yes, there are still men of vision whom God makes His instruments in carrying out Christ's promise that the spirit should lead us into all the truth; and there are still men of that heroic mould in which Stephen and Polycarp were cast, valiant to suffer rather than let the truth suffer, ready to die rather than see Christ betrayed. "My race," said an Armenian woman the other day, half mournfully half proudly, "my race is accustomed to martyrdom." And what is the truth to which these consenting voices bear witness? Under what name are these New Testament men, these martyrs, prophets, and apostles, found praising God? What is it that Holy Church throughout all the world acknowledges? Why simply this, that God is Father, Son, and Holy Ghost—a barren formula, so some insist; the true interpretation, as others believe, of that mystic, Holy, Holy, Holy, under which the Hebrew Church dimly shadowed forth the Christian name of God.

"What dost thou chiefly learn in these Articles of thy Belief?" asks the Catechist of the child who has just been repeating the Apostles' Creed.

"First, I learn," answers the child, "to believe in God the Father, who hath made me and all the world.

"Secondly, in God the Son, who hath redeemed me and all mankind.

"Thirdly, in God the Holy Ghost, who sanctifieth me and all the people of God."

Sonorous language this; and a good commentary on the words,

> The Father of an infinite Majesty;
> Thine adorable true and only Son;
> Also the Holy Ghost the Comforter.

II. Our study of the first portion of the Te Deum, the act of worship as I called it, is done. We pass to the second section, the act of faith.

Thou art the King of Glory; O Christ.
Thou art the everlasting Son: of the Father.
When thou tookest upon thee to deliver man: thou didst humble
    thyself to be born of a Virgin.

When thou hadst overcome the sharpness of death: thou didst open the Kingdom of Heaven to all believers.
Thou sittest at the right hand of God: in the glory of the Father.
We believe that thou shalt come: to be our Judge.
We therefore pray thee help thy servants: whom thou hast redeemed with thy precious blood.
Make them to be numbered with thy Saints: in glory everlasting.

You see at a glance how this passage, taken by itself, is a complete whole, with a dignified beginning and an equally dignified ending. It is a hymn to Christ couched in strongly dogmatic terms. I see no reason why it should not be regarded as the probable core or nucleus around which the Te Deum grew up into what it is, just as the Apostles' Creed grew up around the baptismal formula and the Gloria in Excelsis around the Christmas Angels' hymn. In the famous letter which Pliny the younger wrote to the Emperor Trajan, a document of surpassing interest because among the earliest of those that throw light upon the life of the primitive Church from outside sources, the writer speaks of certain Christians whom he had put under arrest as follows:

"They affirm that the whole of their fault or error lay in this—that they were wont to meet together on a stated day before it was light, and sing among themselves alternately a hymn to Christ as to God, and bind themselves by an oath not to the commission of any wickedness, but not to be guilty of theft or robbery or adultery, never to falsify their word, nor to deny a pledge committed to them when called upon to redeem it. When these things were performed, it was their custom to separate and then to come together again to a meal which they ate in common without any disorder; but this they had forborne since the publication of my edict, by which, according to your command, I prohibited assemblies."

There would seem to be nothing violent in the supposition that this, " Thou art the King of Glory," which, as we have seen, constitutes the very heart of the Te Deum, may have been, in one or another form, the identical hymn to Christ as God, the antiphonal singing of which Pliny so naively describes as constituting the central feature of the Church's Morning Prayer. It need not be insisted that in every part of the Empire the hymn was sung in precisely the same words; to verbal uniformity of that sort not even the Apostles' Creed itself can lay claim. Our historic sense is satisfied if, in a general way, we are permitted to trace connection between this central theme of the Te Deum and the hymn which Pliny's Christians sang, there in far Bithynia at break of day. We resume our study of the text. The expression, " King of Glory," comes from the 24th Psalm, and there can be no doubt whatever as to the purport of it in its author's mind. " Who is this King of Glory? " asks the Psalmist, after having bidden the everlasting doors lift that He may enter; " Who is this King of Glory? " And this is the answer with which he himself supplies us, " The Lord of Hosts, He is the King of Glory."

These salutatory words, therefore, with which the Rex gloriæ Christe opens, bear a clear witness that the hymn is indeed, as Pliny said, addressed to Christ as God. The note of divinity is unmistakably struck. And the next verse, the fifteenth, carries it on, " Thou art the everlasting Son of the Father." Here the word in the Latin is *sempiternus*, which does not necessarily connote eternity, though in no measure inconsistent with that thought. *Sempiternus* means precisely what the English of the Prayer Book makes it mean, namely, lasting forever, and if the verse stood alone there would be nothing to forbid our putting an Arian interpretation upon it. " Yes," one might say, " the Sonship is to last forever, that is true; but, all the same, it began in time. That it is to be 'to everlasting' does not necessarily prove that 'from everlasting' it has been."

But the very next verse reads as if it had been designed of set purpose to protect us against any such misunderstanding of the hymn's teaching as this, for it runs, "When thou tookest upon thee to deliver man: thou didst humble thyself to be born of a Virgin." Had the Son of Mary not been pre-existent before His coming here, He could not thus deliberately have given Himself in advance to the accomplishment of a formed and settled purpose.

True, it may be urged that pre-existence does not of itself necessarily imply eternal pre-existence; but against this objection it is enough to set the general tone of the whole hymn, which the compilers of the King's Chapel Liturgy would not have found it necessary to Arianize had it been Arian already.

But we must not pass this sixteenth verse without taking notice of a very interesting variation in the text. In the version preserved to us in an old Irish Service-book known as the Bangor Antiphonary and now on the shelves of the Ambrosian Library at Milan, instead of the reading

TE DEUM LAUDAMUS.

"When thou tookest upon thee to deliver man," we have, "When thou tookest upon thee man, in order that thou mightest deliver the world." This suggests that fine phrase in the Athanasian Creed, the "taking of the manhood into God," and as a side-light upon the true and full significance of the verse as we have it is very valuable. Certain critics of the recent revision of the Prayer Book who scent "Americanism" at every turn are sorry that the language of the latter half of this verse was not restored, when we had the opportunity in hand, to the form familiar to us in the English Book; but to this it is a sufficient reply to observe that in modern English the verb "abhor" has acquired a tinge of meaning that did not attach to it when it was first used as the equivalent of the Latin "horreo," a word wholly devoid, I am safe in saying, of that suggestion of hatred or disgust which is inseparable from "abhor" as we employ it in present-day speech.

In the next verse we have a deeply interesting reminiscence of St. Paul. "When thou hadst overcome the sharpness of death: thou didst open the Kingdom of Heaven to all believers." In place of this abstract word "sharpness," signifying a quality, put the concrete noun "needle" or "sting," and you will have not only a more accurate translation of the Latin *aculeus*, but also a singularly helpful clew to the real meaning of the verse. For what is the needle or sting of death? As often as we have taken part in the solemn burial office of the Church we have heard it clearly defined. "The sting of death is sin." That is the goad which Thanatos, prince of the nether world, carries in his hand for bauble. So then what Christ overcame upon the cross, was not merely, as the careless reader of this verse might infer, the anguish of dissolution, it was the power of sin. He thus cuts away, like the prince in the legend, the dense thicket that has blocked approach to the royal palace, slays the dragon, and opens the Kingdom of Heaven to all believers. You notice how wonderfully the sentence, when thus interpreted, chimes in with the following passage from the second chapter of the Epistle to the Hebrews. "Forasmuch then as the children are partakers of flesh and blood, he also himself likewise took part of the same" (humbled himself to be born of a Virgin), "that through death he might destroy him that hath the power of death, that is the devil, and deliver them who through fear of death were all their life-time subject to bondage." The dogmatic harmony of the two passages could scarcely be made more complete.

" Thou sittest at the right hand of God in the glory of the Father." We are not to lay stress upon the sitting posture as signifying anything more than simply the plenitude of power. The session does not mean inactivity; what it really symbolizes is puissance, majesty. The throne or chair is the emblem of a strength so strong that it can exert itself without apparent effort. Stephen, at the climax of his impassioned speech before his judges, sees Jesus, not sitting, but standing at the right hand of God. And so the Church emphasizes its freedom from the deadness of the letter both of the Creed and of the Te Deum by bidding us address the Lord Christ on St. Stephen's Day as one who *standeth* " at the right hand of God to succor all those who suffer for him."

Yes, it would bode ill for Christendom were He who is its Prince and Leader sitting idly by upon a sapphire throne a calm observer of our battle, a quiet critic of our struggle and no more. So Epicurean an interpretation of the great doctrine of Christ's session at the right hand of God would be discouraging indeed. Such a picture has altogether too much in common with the old Olympic conception of the gods as segregated in their selfish heaven—" careless of mankind."

For they lie beside their nectar and the bolts are hurled
Far below them in the valleys, and the clouds are lightly curled
Round their golden houses.

Nothing like that, we may be sure, can truthfully be said of the heaven where Christ lives seated and regnant at the right hand of God. It were blasphemy to think of Him as so self-centred in His own beatitude that He can

Smile in secret looking over wasted lands,
Blight and famine, plague and earthquake, roaring deeps and fiery sands,
Clanging fights and flaming towns and sinking ships and praying hands.

No, He is there not to enjoy the apathy of an ignoble rest, but to stretch forth the right hand of His majesty to be our defence against all our enemies. Not only so, but the hour draws near when we are to know this. At evening-time it shall be light, and even now the clouded day of man's long pilgrimage begins to brighten, and in the glow of sunset there is heard his closing strophe of the " Hymn to Christ as God "—

TE DEUM LAUDAMUS. 189

We believe that thou shalt come to be our Judge.
We therefore pray thee, help thy servants, whom thou hast redeemed with thy precious blood.
Make them to be numbered with thy Saints in glory everlasting.

"Therefore" is an unusual word in hymns. It savors more of what is logical than of what is metrical. And yet if it be logic that we have here it is logic of a sort that finds its parallel in that most rythmical of formularies, the Litany, for there, as here, we see prayer based upon a solid substratum of historic fact as its reason why. In the Litany we intercede with Christ because of what happened in His earthly life and plead before Him all the memories of the incarnation.

"By thine agony and bloody sweat, by thy Cross and Passion; by thy precious Death and Burial; by thy glorious Resurrection and Ascension . . . Good Lord deliver us."

How differs this from, Thou tookest upon thee to deliver man; Thou didst overcome; Thou hast opened the kingdom, Thou dost sit at the right hand, We believe that thou shalt come—

Therefore, therefore, we pray thee, help thy servants. The parallelism is complete.

III. The third and final section of the Te Deum is supplicatory in its character, and is, as

I have already intimated, mainly made up of quotations from the Psalms.

> O Lord save thy people ; and bless Thine heritage,
> Govern them and lift them up forever.

This, you observe, is a very close paraphrase of the last verse of the twenty-eighth Psalm, which in King James's version, runs, " Save thy people and bless thine inheritance, rule them also and lift them up forever," and in the versicles which follow upon the Creed in our Order for Evening Prayer we catch the same note.

The one hundred and forty-fifth Psalm gives us, in its second verse, the original of what follows next, for the resemblance between " Every day will I give thanks unto thee and praise thy name for ever and ever," to " Day by day we magnify thee, and we worship thy Name: ever, world without end " is too close to have been accidental.

Thomas Hobbes of Malmesbury, the curmudgeon among moralists, but a past master of word-fence, draws a nice distinction between praising and magnifying. " The form of speech," he says, " whereby men signify their opinion of the goodness of anything is praise; that whereby they signify the power and greatness of anything is magnifying." It is characteristic of the Te Deum that these two strains are blended in it throughout. God is magnified in His character of Creator, and praised in His character of Redeemer. The song is a song both of Moses and of the Lamb. "Great and marvellous are thy works, Lord God Almighty," is the one strain. "Just and true are thy ways, thou King of saints," is the other.

The next verse, "Vouchsafe, O Lord, to keep us this day without sin," suggests the Lord's Prayer, and the next after that, "O Lord have mercy upon us, have mercy upon us," the third verse of the Psalm, "Unto thee lift I up mine eyes, O thou that dwellest in the heavens."

The 28th verse, "O Lord, let thy mercy be upon us, as our trust is in thee," breathes the spirit of the Psalms even though it may not be traceable to any definite original. It is found in a slightly altered form in the English Litany, where it directly precedes the Lord's prayer.

And now that we have reached the last verse of the Te Deum, I bid you notice the very striking transition which is effected in it from the first person plural to the first person singular. "We" it has been hitherto, but now, "O Lord in thee have I trusted, I shall never be confounded."

In this respect the Te Deum is in marked contrast with the Miserere, which is throughout the utterance of the individual soul until the very end, when it breaks out with a recognition of the Church, " O be favorable and gracious unto Sion." The Te Deum, on the other hand, starts in upon the churchly or social key, and takes no note whatsoever of the individual until the close. Up to this point all has been, as we may say, multitudinous. The picture before our eyes has been a panorama of the armies of the living God. But now, at the very end, we catch the cry of the single solitary soul. Stealing away from her association with the unnumbered and innumerable host, forgetful for the moment of all in the wide universe save her Maker and herself, she cries, " O Lord in Thee, Thee whom the angels and archangels hymn, Thee to whom Heavens and Powers, Cherubs and Seraphs cry, Thee whom Apostles praise, and Prophets and Martyrs and the Holy Church, in Thee have I, poor, insignificant, worthless little I, in Thee have I trusted. I shall not be forever perplexed."

That " I shall not be forever perplexed " is a

more accurate rendering of *non confundar in æternum*, than "Let me never be confounded" all scholars must acknowledge. And how much it adds to the devotional value of the hymn when we permit it thus to culminate in an indomitable trust. It is in the spirit of Job's "Though he slay me, yet will I trust in him." "Distressed I may be," the singer seems to say, "harassed by anxieties, compassed about with fears, beset by doubts and by misgivings, nevertheless, I know whom I have believed, God has never failed me in the past, and it simply cannot be that to eternity I shall have dimness for my portion and my lot. No, no, O Lord, in thee have I trusted, I shall not for ever be confounded." And so Te Deum ends in what good Jeremy Taylor calls, "the confidence of a certain faith, the comfort of a reasonable, religious, and holy hope."

Do you complain that I have pulled the song to pieces and by too rigid an analysis have dismembered what you have always found pleasure in accounting one self-consistent whole? That may be the temporary impression left by our study of the text, but I cannot believe that it will be the permanent and final one. The time will come, and that soon, when the real unity of the hymn will seem to you all the more marvellous because of your having acquainted yourself with its diversity.

A trilogy has oneness back of its threeness; it would not be a trilogy if it had not. And so what I have called the act of praise, the act of faith, and the act of prayer, blend into unity the moment it is discerned that all three of them are fastened by indissoluble bonds to the great central truth of the Incarnation of the Son of God.

Unity? Yes, the Te Deum has unity, the very best sort of unity. What gives an old Gothic Cathedral, Lincoln, Canterbury, or York, unity? Most assuredly not the fact of the original design's having sprung complete out of the brain of a definite person known to history, for that is just the thing that did not happen. To name the architect of any one of these three famous Churches would be as impossible as it is to-day to name the author of the Te Deum. The mediæval Cathedral was a growth.

In such a building we discern precisely the same composite character as respects structural origins that we have noticed in our hymn. Examine the building in detail, follow your guide into every side-chapel, every retiring angle, every groined recess, and you will feel as if variety and inconsistency were inwrought into the very being of the fabric. The nave, it may be, is Norman, the transepts Early English, the choir late perpendicular. One pious Bishop, you are told, added this peculiarity, another, his successor, added that. At each step the eye falls on something different and the impression received is one of utter incongruity. But when you have done with your analytic examination of the edifice, go and take your stand at the great western entrance and forgetting all thought of detail, endeavor to apprehend and to appreciate the whole beautiful idea. See it as it lies before you one mighty cross of stone. Look through the long vista walled and arched like an avenue of ice-encrusted elms, note the great bars of sunlight falling slant across the spaces of the distant choir. And if at that moment the voice of some musical response, some snatch of Psalm or Litany happen to strike your ear, you will feel the influence of a unity indescribable and the building, from having seemed the handiwork of many men and divers generations, will become to you beholding it simply the present temple of the ever-living God. Of such sort is the unity of the Te Deum.

It seems scarcely necessary to say that the Church Club is not responsible for any individual opinions on points not ruled by the Church, which the learned theologians who have been good enough to lecture under its auspices may have expressed.